Thinking About How Our World Really Works

David Downs

Thinking About How Our World Really Works
Copyright © 2022 by David Downs
Eagle, Idaho

All rights reserved including the right of reproduction in whole or in part in any form.

Library of Congress Control Number: 2022913876
ISBN: 979-8-9863515-1-3 (paperback)
ISBN: 979-8-9863515-2-0 (e-book)
1. Self-improvement 2. Critical thinking 3. Choices 4. Life

Designed by Mary Ann Smith

Printed in the United States of America
First Edition: 2022

to the memory of Doris

my friend, spouse, partner, mentor

TABLE OF CONTENTS

Introduction 6

Other introductory thoughts 9

Nature 10

Life 16

Humanity 22

Civilization 26

Learning and Knowledge 30

Thinking and Understanding 36

Fact or Opinion 42

Reality or Fantasy 44

Cognition and Emotion 48

Change 52

Cause and Effect 56

Self 60

Purpose 66

Choices 70

Happiness 76

Morality 80

Character and Principles.. 86

Attitude and Behavior.. 92

Balance and Alignment... 102

Realist or Idealist... 112

Worth and Value.. 120

Society.. **124**

Social Order... 132

Culture... 140

Individualism or Collectivism... 146

Power and Control... 152

Authoritarianism.. 158

Honorable or Corrupt... 166

Deceit.. 172

Progress and Prosperity.. 182

Meritocracy.. 190

Glossary.. **196**

INTRODUCTION

This book is perhaps unlike any book you have seen before. Maybe even calling it a book is a bit misleading.

It is not structured the same as self-help and self-improvement books typically are structured. Except for encouraging rational and logical thinking about how our world really works, it does not contain any do-this or do-that advice. And it is not meant to promote any spiritual, social, or political point of view. But it is "a bound text in printed form." So we will call it a book.

At its most basic level, this book is about how we, as individual human beings, choose or fail to choose how we live our lives. Whether we like it or not, the reality of things is that life is a natural competition between an untold number of players that proceeds according to an infinite number of constantly changing rules. So it really is not surprising that we sometimes find that life is hard. Yet, as we all probably have noticed, life seems less hard for some people than for others.

Why is this so? Are there ways to play the game of life that make our lives easier and more rewarding? Is there something the more fortunate people know that the less fortunate have not yet discovered? Could it be that those who are the more fortunate have learned that their lives become easier when they make mostly wise decisions, and also that the more fully they understand how the world really works, the more likely it is that they make wise decisions?

This book provides a series of self-paced and open-ended exercises that are designed to help you better understand these often complex and complicated matters. For some or maybe many readers, this will not be a read once and understand book. It perhaps instead will become something of a read and discover; read, learn, and think; and then finally, read and understand study guide.

The exercises it contains are organized around an ordered list of broad concepts that will direct your thinking first toward the world we live in, then, to our place in this world, and finally, to our interdependencies with other people.

It seems that many people, especially during their formative years, rarely think about these things, except maybe in a very limited and personal way. This results in some of them falling prey to propaganda and other similarly dishonest but brutally effective methods of thought control.

At the beginning of each chapter are one or more definitions of words or terms which frame and describe a particular concept that relates to how we live our lives. Next, in most chapters, are additional defined terms that in some way are related to the primary concept. You may notice that some of these terms are included in more than one chapter. This is because many of these concepts and ideas are interrelated and, frequently, interdependent.

Each chapter then presents some questions that are designed to further expand your learning and thinking. At the end of each chapter is a quick reference mini-glossary of words used in that chapter.

A comprehensive glossary containing many words and terms used in this book is provided as its last chapter. For some, this glossary may be the most important thing in the book.

Words, of course, function as carriers of meaning that enable learning and thinking. So it follows, the more words you know, the greater your ability to learn and think. And the more precisely you define the words in your vocabulary, the more precisely you are able to think.

The definitions provided here generally are contextual definitions. That is, their meanings are determined by the words that surround them. Look in any dictionary and you will find additional and different definitions for most of these words.

This book was written both to encourage more thinking for oneself about how our world really works, and also to encourage and assist you, its readers, to develop or improve your abilities to think critically and make wise decisions. Hopefully, it, for each of you, will meet both of these objectives.

"You can avoid reality, but you cannot avoid the consequences of avoiding reality."

—Ayn Rand

"The past is irrevocably fixed, so all options are present or future."

—Thomas Sowell

"... in the end everyone stands alone; and the important thing is, who it is that stands alone ..."

—Arthur Schopenhauer

"Start where you are. Use what you have. Do what you can."

—Arthur Ashe

"I have no regrets because I know I did my best ..."

—Midori Ito

NATURE

the material world and its phenomena

LAWS OF NATURE
the uniformity of natural instincts, actions, and relationships of organic beings

COMPETITION
a rivalry for supremacy or advantage

SUCCESS
favorable or desirable outcome

FAILURE
unfavorable or undesirable outcome

RESPONSIBLE
accountable for own conduct; dependable and trustworthy

IRRESPONSIBLE

not accountable for own conduct; not dependable or trustworthy

PREDATOR

one that injures, exploits, or plunders others

PREY

one that is the victim of another

OPPOSITES

a duality of complementary or mutually exclusive things

---

1. Do you or do you not think that self-preservation is the most basic instinct of all living beings? Why?

2. Do you think there are other concepts that better summarize the laws of nature than competition and success or failure? If so, what do you think they are?

3. Do you believe that success generally is earned or just happens? Why?

4. Do you think there is anything more central to the laws of nature than individual responsibility? Why or why not?

5. Do you think there is anything more fundamental to the laws of nature than the existence of opposites? Why or why not?

6. To what extent and in what ways do you think human behavior is influenced by the laws of nature?

accountable – subject to an obligation to report, explain, or justify one's behavior

action – something done or accomplished

basic – constituting, forming, or serving as a base element or starting point

behavior – the way one acts or conducts oneself

being – the fact of existence; a living thing

believe – to accept the truth, existence, or validity of something

central – principal or dominant thing on which related things depend

competition – a rivalry for supremacy or advantage

complementary – the characteristic of what enables a person or thing to enhance the strengths and compensate for the weaknesses of another

concept – a generalized or abstract notion or understanding of something

conduct – personal behavior, way of acting, or bearing or deportment

dependable – consistently behaves or acts in an expected and sensible way

desirable – worth wanting, doing, or achieving

duality – the condition of having or combining two different or opposite things

earned – acquired in exchange for work done

exploit – to selfishly take advantage of

existence – the state or fact of having actual being at a particular point in time

extent – the range, distance, space, or magnitude of something

failure – unfavorable or undesirable outcome

favorable – helpful, tending to promote or facilitate

fundamental – forming or serving as an essential component of a concept, system, or structure

human – reference to the species *homo sapiens*

individual – reference to a single human being or other single distinct entity

influence – a power to change a someone's belief or behavior or to affect a course of events without exerting direct control or apparent effort

instinct – an innate response to specific stimuli, how one naturally behaves, thinks, or feels

injure – to cause harm or inflict damage

irresponsible – not accountable for own conduct

laws of nature – the uniformity of natural instincts, actions, and relationships of organic beings

material – something that is used or that can be used to make something

mutually exclusive – not possible to occur or exist at the same time

natural – existing in or formed by nature

nature – the material world and its phenomena

opposites – a duality of complementary or mutually exclusive things

organic – pertaining to or derived from living beings

outcome – a consequence, end result, or final product

phenomenon – an observable fact or event

plunder – to steal or take wrongfully

predator – one that injures, exploits, or plunders others

prey – one that is the victim of another

relationship – the state of being related or interrelated; a connection, association, or involvement

responsibility – the condition of being obligated to deal with something or being accountable for something

responsible – accountable for own conduct; dependable and trustworthy

self-preservation – the basic instinct of preserving one's own existence

success – favorable or desirable outcome

think – to use one's mind to remember, ponder, imagine, plan, decide, or otherwise produce thought

trustworthy – deserving of trust or confidence

uniform – always the same, identical or consistent in form, manner, or degree

victim – one that is harmed by another

world – the earthly state of human existence

LIFE

aspect of organic existence which grows and evolves; the span of time an organism is alive; all of the experiences and actions that constitute a person's existence

---

ECONOMIC
relating to production, distribution, and consumption of goods and services

PERSONAL RESOURCES
the physical body, mind, energy, and time that are naturally and uniquely possessed by each human being

EFFICIENT
the degree of success in doing something with least waste of time and energy

EFFECTIVE

the degree of success in producing a desired result

ADVERSITY

bad luck or unfavorable fortune or fate

FAIR

absence of bias, impartial

---

1. Does it or does it not seem to you correct to think of each person, or for that matter, each living thing, as a discrete economic unit? Why?

2. How efficiently and effectively do you think you are using each of your personal resources, namely your body, mind, energy, and time? On what do you base this assessment?

3. Do you or do you not think adversity is an unavoidable fact of life? Why?

4. Do you think the statement "life isn't fair" is actually true? Why or why not?

---

absence – the condition of not being present

action – something done or accomplished

actual – existing in fact or reality

adversity – bad luck or unfavorable fortune or fate

allocate – to assign or set apart

alternative – one of two or more choices or courses of action

aspect – a particular characteristic or feature of a person or thing

assessment – the action or product of determining the value, significance, or extent of something

being – a living thing

bias – inclination or tendency to favor one over another

constitute – to make up or form the completeness of something

correct – in agreement with truth or facts, or in compliance with what is generally accepted

degree – any of the series of steps or stages in a progression, process, or course of action

desire – something wanted or wished for

discrete – constituting a separate and distinct thing

economic – relating to production, distribution, and consumption of goods and services

effective – the degree of success in producing a desired result

efficient – the degree of success in doing something with least waste of time and energy

energy – power expended to cause or enable change

evolve – to change or develop gradually

existence – the state or fact of having actual being at a particular point in time

experience – doing, seeing, or feeling something

fact – something that is consistent with objective reality and can be proven to be true

fair – absence of bias, impartial

fate – a power, force, or principle that is believed to cause things to happen as they do

fortune – the chance and unpredictable happening of favorable and unfavorable events

human – a person; reference to the species *homo sapiens*

impartial – lack of preference for one thing over another

life – aspect of organic existence which grows and evolves; the span of time an organism is alive; all of the experiences and actions that constitute a person's existence

luck – the chance happening of good fortune or adversity

mind – the faculty of a person that enables one to perceive, think, remember, desire, and imagine

natural – existing in or formed by nature

organic – pertaining to or derived from living beings

organism – any living thing

person – an individual human being

personal resources – the physical body, mind, energy, and time that are naturally and uniquely possessed by each human being

physical – relating to the material structure of organic beings; having material or concrete existence

possess – to have under one's power or control

produce – to bring about or create

relate – to have connection or reference

resource – something that has utility or that is available for use

result – to occur as a consequence, effect, or conclusion

scarce – small, insignificant, or insufficient amount

statement – a description, assertion, or declaration

think – to use one's mind to remember, ponder, imagine, plan, decide, or otherwise produce thought

time – a non-renewable and ultimately finite resource that can be expended in alternative ways

true – that which exists in accordance with fact or reality

unavoidable – not possible to be avoided, inevitable

unfavorable – not favorable or advantageous

unique – existing as the only one, implies being without a known parallel

unit – an individual, group, structure, or other entity regarded as a primary element of a whole

use – to put into action or service or employ for a purpose

waste – to use or expend needlessly or carelessly

HUMANITY

the whole existence of the human species

PERSON
an individual human being

FAMILY
a group of people who are biologically or legally related to one another

COMMUNITY
a group of people who live in a particular geographical area or who share common interests or points of view

SOCIETY
a system of human organization that supplies protection, continuity, security, and identity

PRIME ELEMENT

fundamental or most critical component of a complex entity

---

1. In what ways do you think one human being is the same as other human beings? In what ways do you think we are similar? In what ways do you think each human being is different?

2. Do you think that people, families, communities, and societies are all essential or beneficial elements of humanity? Why? If you think all are essential or beneficial elements of humanity, which do you think are essential and which do you think are beneficial? Why?

3. Do you consider people, families, communities, or societies to be the prime element of humanity? Why?

---

area – a geographic region, a part of the earth's surface

being – the fact of existence; a living thing

benefit – something that produces helpful results or that promotes or enhances well-being

biological – pertaining to genetic lineage

common – belonging to or shared by members of a group

community – a group of people who live in a particular geographical area or who share common interests or points of view

complex – something that is made up of interdependent parts or elements whose dependencies may be imperfectly known or are unknowable

consider – to regard or believe, or to think carefully about something

continuity – uninterrupted extension in space, time, or sequence

critical – indispensable or vital

different – not alike in nature, form, or quality

distinct – clearly separate and different

element – a constituent part

entity – something that exists as a discrete unit

essential – absolutely necessary, indispensable

existence – the state or fact of having actual being at a particular point in time

family – a group of people who are biologically or legally related to one another

fundamental – forming or serving as an essential component of a concept, system, or structure

geographical – relating to a particular place or area on the earth's surface

group – a number of similar individuals or things considered together as one

human – reference to the species *homo sapiens*

humanity – the whole existence of the human species

identify – to recognize as a particular person or thing

individual – reference to a single human being or other single distinct entity

interest – concern about or involvement with something or someone

legal – relating to or concerned with law; established or recognized by law

live – to be alive or to reside in a particular place

organization – spontaneous or deliberate formation of arrangement or order

particular – reference to a single person or thing rather than to others

person – an individual human being

point of view – the perspective from which we view and explain something

prime element – fundamental or most critical component of a complex entity

protect – to defend or shield against injury, harm, or loss

relate – to have connection or reference

security – free from actual risk or danger

similar – having common but not identical characteristics

society – a system of human organization that supplies protection, continuity, security, and identity

special – exceptional, surpassing what is common or usual

species – a group of closely related animals or plants which have common attributes

supply – to provide or make available

system – interacting, interrelated, or interdependent elements that form or function as a whole

whole – all aspects of a thing, something in its entirety

CIVILIZATION

advanced stage of human social and economic development and organization

---

THRIVE
to be successful or to flourish

SURVIVE
to remain alive

INNOVATION
change that creates a new dimension of performance

PRODUCTIVITY
the quality, state, or fact of being able to create, enhance, or provide goods and services

STANDARD OF LIVING

the level of material comfort experienced by a person

or group of people

---

1. What do you think is the principal reason civilizations come into existence?

2. Why do you think that even highly advanced civilizations have collapsed and ceased to exist?

3. Do you think our civilization could collapse and cease to exist? Why or why not?

---

advanced – being at a higher level or more highly developed

change – the act or instance of becoming different

civilization – advanced stage of human social and economic development and organization

comfort – the condition or cause of feeling pleasurable ease or relief

cost – money or other resource expended to acquire, produce, or maintain something

create – to cause to exist or bring into being

develop – to grow into or bring to a more mature, advanced, or effective state

dimension – one of a set of elements or factors that constitute a complete existence, personality, or consciousness

economic – relating to production, distribution, and consumption of goods and services

enhance – to improve the quality or value of something

exist – to have actual being at a particular point in time

existence – the state or fact of having actual being at a particular point in time

experience – doing, seeing, or feeling something

fact – something that is consistent with objective reality and can be proven to be true

flourish – to do well or be in a vigorous state

goods and services – reference to tangible items such as commodities, equipment, materials, or supplies (goods) and work that is done on behalf of or for the benefit of others (services)

human – reference to the species *homo sapiens*

innovation – change that creates a new dimension of performance

material – having importance or consequence

multiple – more than one

organization – spontaneous or deliberate formation of arrangement or order

performance – action of doing something or competence demonstrated when doing it

principal – most important or consequential

produce – to bring about or create

productivity – the quality, state, or fact of being able to create, enhance, or provide goods and services

provide – to make available or to supply

quality – a characteristic or the essential nature of a person or thing; level of excellence

reason – the basis or motive for an action, decision, or belief

social – relating to the way people live together and interact with others

stage – one of a series of steps or positions

standard of living – the level of material comfort experienced by a person or group of people

state – the whole being of something

success – accomplishment of something desired, planned, or attempted

survive – to remain alive

think – to use one's mind to remember, ponder, imagine, plan, decide, or otherwise produce thought

thrive – to be successful or to flourish

wealthy – the state or condition of having significant resources

work – mental or physical effort expended to accomplish or produce something

LEARNING

to acquire knowledge or skill or to become aware and informed

KNOWLEDGE

information acquired through experience, schooling, or study

INCREMENTAL
denoting a usually small positive or negative change in a variable quantity

CUMULATIVE
sum of incremental amounts

IGNORANT
having no knowledge, the condition of being unaware or uninformed

INFORMED
the condition of being aware, knowledgeable, or educated

KNOWN
perceived or understood with clarity or certainty; the condition of having familiarity or knowledge

UNKNOWN
not within the scope of one's knowledge, experience, or understanding

UNKNOWABLE
impossible to know, existing beyond the capacities of human cognition or knowledge

TIME AND PLACE
unique and virtually immeasurable number of combinations of points in time and space

---

1. What do you think are the implications of learning being incremental and cumulative?
2. Do you think that we all are ignorant about most things? Why or why not?

3. What are things that you consider to be known, unknown, and unknowable?

4. Do you think that time and place affect what is known, unknown, and unknowable? Why or why not?

---

acquire – to gain or come into ownership or possession of something

affect – to act on or cause change

aware – having or showing realization or perception

capacity – the potential to learn or retain knowledge

certainty – the quality of being known or proven to be true

change – the act or instance of becoming different

clarity – clearness or lucidity as to perception or understanding

cognition – mental activity of acquiring, recalling, or using knowledge

combine – the act of joining or mixing two or more things to form a separate thing

condition – a state of existence as determined by a set of circumstances

consider – to regard or believe, or to think carefully about something

cumulative – sum of incremental amounts

education – the action or process of teaching and learning; the knowledge, skills, values, beliefs, and habits learned from observation, study, and experience

exist – to have actual being at a particular point in time

experience – doing, seeing, or feeling something

familiar – acquainted, often encountered or seen

function – the specific action or purpose for which a person or thing is designed, used, or exists

human – reference to the species Homo sapiens

ignorant – having no knowledge, the condition of being unaware or uninformed

implication – the effect a decision, action, or event is logically expected to have on something else

impossible – cannot exist or occur

incremental – denoting a usually small positive or negative change in a variable quantity

information – facts or ideas received or given

informed – the condition of being aware, knowledgeable, or educated

knowledge – information acquired through experience, schooling, or study

known – perceived or understood with clarity or certainty; the condition of having familiarity or knowledge

learn – to acquire knowledge or skill or to become aware and informed

negative – characterized by subtraction or decrease

perceive – to sense, recognize, realize, or understand

positive – characterized by increase or addition

quantity – the amount or total number of something

relative – considered in comparison or relation to something else

scope – extent of consideration, activity, or influence

skill – learned ability to do something in an efficient and capable way

space – the three-dimensional area in which all matter exists

study – applying the mind to the acquisition of knowledge through reading, observation, or research

think – to use one's mind to remember, ponder, imagine, plan, decide, or otherwise produce thought

time – a non-renewable and ultimately finite resource that can be expended in alternative ways

time and place – unique and virtually immeasurable number of combinations of points in time and space

understanding – the condition or quality of having the ability to comprehend and judge the nature and significance of something

unique – existing as the only one, implies being without a known parallel

unknowable – impossible to know, existing beyond the capacities of human cognition or knowledge

unknown – not within the scope of one's knowledge, experience, or understanding

variable – the quality of being able or likely to change

virtually – in fact or for all practical purposes; almost but not quite, nearly

THINKING

the act of using one's mind to produce thought

UNDERSTANDING

the condition or quality of having the ability to comprehend and judge the nature and significance of something

---

LOGICAL THINKING
cognition that is fact-based and logical

FAULTY THINKING
a biased or illogical way of using one's mind

ABSTRACT THINKING

ability to think in terms of principles and generalizations

CONCRETE THINKING

cognition centered on objects or ideas as specific items rather than as principles and generalizations

---

1. Do you or do you not think concrete thinking can sometimes cause faulty thinking? Why?

2. Do you think one can learn more about human behavior by studying history, economics, and biology or by studying sociology and psychology? Why?

3. To what extent do you think you currently know about how our world really works? On what do you base your opinion?

---

ability – the capacity, knowledge, and skill to do something

abstract thinking – ability to think in terms of principles and generalizations

act – to do something

behavior – the way one acts or conducts oneself

biased – having or showing an unjust or unfair opinion or feeling about someone or something

biology – the study of organisms and their life processes

cause – something that brings about something else

cognition – mental activity of acquiring, recalling, or using knowledge

comprehend – to grasp or perceive the nature or meaning of something

concrete thinking – cognition centered on objects or ideas as specific items rather than as principles and generalizations

condition – a state of existence as determined by a set of circumstances

current – occurring in or existing at the present time

economics – the study of how allocations and uses of scarce resources affect human behavior and well-being

extent – the range, distance, space, or magnitude of something

fact – something that is consistent with objective reality and can be proven to be true

faulty thinking – a biased or illogical way of using one's mind

generalization – a statement that summarizes an idea or impression

history – the study of past events and how they relate to human behavior

human – reference to the species *homo sapiens*

idea – a thought or opinion that is the product of mental understanding, awareness, or activity

illogical – contradicting or disregarding the principles of logic

immeasurable – impossible to measure or without known limits

inaccurate – incorrect or untrue

judge – to form an opinion after careful consideration

know – to perceive or understand with clarity or certainty

learn – to acquire knowledge or skill or to become aware and informed

logical – relating to or in accordance with reasoning that involves correct or reliable inference

logical thinking – cognition that is fact-based and logical

mind – the faculty of a person that enables one to perceive, think, remember, desire, and imagine

nature – the inherent character or basic constitution of a person or thing

need – something that is required or necessary

object – the focus of attention, feeling, thought, or action

opinion – belief about something that may or may not be based on fact or knowledge

principle – a fundamental truth that serves as a foundational tenet of a system of beliefs or a chain of reasoning

produce – to bring about or create

psychology – the study of individual human thought and behavior

quality – a characteristic or the essential nature of a person or thing

significant – important and deserving of attention

sociology – the study of human social behavior

specific – relating to a particular person or thing

study – applying the mind to the acquisition of knowledge through reading, observation, or research

term – a word or expression that when used contextually has precise meaning

think – to use one's mind to remember, ponder, imagine, plan, decide, or otherwise produce thought

thinking – the act of using one's mind to produce thought

understanding – the condition or quality of having the ability to comprehend and judge the nature and significance of something

use – to put into action or service or employ for a purpose

work – to function or operate

world – the earthly state of human existence

FACT

something that is consistent with objective reality and can be proven to be true

OPINION

belief about something that may or may not be based on fact or knowledge

---

1. Do you think it is important that personal opinions be fact-based? Why or why not?

2. To what extent do you think your own opinions are fact-based? On what do you base your assessment?

---

assessment – the action or product of determining the value, significance, or extent of something

belief – a person's conviction about the truth, existence, or validity of something

believe – to accept the truth, existence, or validity of something

consistent – free from variation

extent – the range, distance, space, or magnitude of something

fact – something that is consistent with objective reality and can be proven to be true

important – something that is necessary or that has significant worth or value

knowledge – information acquired through experience, schooling, or study

objective – the quality or condition of not being influenced by personal beliefs or feelings in considering and representing facts

opinion – belief about something that may or may not be based on fact or knowledge

personal – anything that relates or pertains to an individual person's own self

reality – the state of things as they actually are rather than as they are imagined or desired to be

think – to use one's mind to remember, ponder, imagine, plan, decide, or otherwise produce thought

total – the whole amount or complete scope of something

true – that which exists in accordance with fact or reality

REALITY

the state of things as they actually are
rather than as they are imagined or desired to be

FANTASY

something that is created by and exists only
in the imagination

TIME AND PLACE

unique and virtually immeasurable number of combinations of
points in time and space

ILLUSION

a mistaken perception of reality

DELUSION
belief in something that is false

RESPONSIBLE
dependable and trustworthy

---

1. How do you think that what exists is affected by time and place?

2. In what ways do you think being individually responsible can be affected by illusion or delusion?

---

accountable – subject to an obligation to report, explain, or justify one's behavior

actual – existing in fact or reality

affect – to act on or cause change

belief – a person's conviction about the truth, existence, or validity of something

combine – the act of joining or mixing two or more things to form a separate thing

create – to cause to exist or bring into being

delusion – belief in something that is false

dependable – consistently behaves or acts in an expected and sensible way

desire – something wanted or wished for

exist – to have actual being at a particular point in time

false – contrary to fact or truth

fantasy – something that is created by and exists only in the imagination

illusion – a mistaken perception of reality

imagination – the faculty to form a mental perception of something that has never before been known to actually exist

imagine – the act or instance of forming a perception of something in one's mind

immeasurable – impossible to measure or without known limits

individual – reference to a single human being or other single distinct entity

perception – comprehension or understanding of something

reality – the state of things as they actually are rather than as they are imagined or desired to be

responsible – accountable for own conduct; dependable and trustworthy

space – the three-dimensional area in which all matter exists

state – the whole being of something

think – to use one's mind to remember, ponder, imagine, plan, decide, or otherwise produce thought

time – a non-renewable and ultimately finite resource that can be expended in alternative ways

time and place – unique and virtually immeasurable number of combinations of points in time and space

trustworthy – deserving of trust or confidence

unique – existing as the only one, implies being without a known parallel

virtually – in fact or for all practical purposes; almost but not quite, nearly

COGNITION

mental activity of acquiring, recalling, or using knowledge

EMOTION

a spontaneous mental reaction experienced as a strong feeling

---

ANALYTIC THINKING
way of thinking that is based on systematic analysis of data or situation

INTUITION
what one feels to be true or correct, often without any conscious reasoning or proof

1. Which important decisions that most people face during their lives do you think should be made using mostly analytic thinking and which should be made mostly based on intuition? Why?

2. What role, if any, do you think emotion or intuition should have in analytic thinking? Why?

3. Do you think that making good decisions can require both analytical thinking and intuition? Why or why not?

---

acquire – to gain or come into ownership or possession of something

activity – something requiring physical or mental effort that one or many engage in doing

analysis – careful and methodical thought

analytic thinking – way of thinking that is based on systematic analysis of data or situation

cognition – mental activity of acquiring, recalling, or using knowledge

conscious – focused on or being aware of something in particular

correct – in agreement with truth or facts, or in compliance with what is generally accepted

decision – act of resolving a question or issue or of choosing between two or more courses of action

emotion – a spontaneous mental reaction experienced as a strong feeling

experience – doing, seeing, or feeling something

feeling – an emotional state or reaction

good – satisfactory as to quality, quantity, or degree

important – something that is necessary or that has significant worth or value

intuition – what one feels to be true or correct, often without any conscious reasoning or proof

knowledge – information acquired through experience, schooling, or study

mental – relating to the mind

reaction – the natural or learned response to various stimuli

reasoning – using one's mind to think, understand, and form judgments

rely – to depend on or place trust in

required – stipulated as absolutely indispensable

role – functional part or element of something

senses – faculties, such as sight, hearing, smell, taste, or touch, by which humans perceive external and internal stimuli

situation – a state of affairs

spontaneous – happening or arising without apparent external cause

systematic – methodical, characterized by thoroughness and regularity

think – to use one's mind to remember, ponder, imagine, plan, decide, or otherwise produce thought

true – that which exists in accordance with fact or reality

understanding – the condition or quality of having the ability to comprehend and judge the nature and significance of something

use – to put into action or service or employ for a purpose

CHANGE

the act or instance of becoming different

INEVITABLE
impossible to avoid or prevent, certain to happen

CONSTANT
continuously occurring or recurring

DISRUPTIVE
causing disorder, turmoil, or an interruption in the way something usually is done or happens

INVIGORATING
the quality of having an enlivening or stimulating effect

---

1. Do you think it is correct to consider change as inevitable, constant, disruptive, and invigorating? Why or why not?

2. In what ways do you perceive living conditions where you live to have changed during the past one hundred years? Is your perception of what has changed fact-based? What do you think caused or enabled these changes?

---

act – to do something

avoid – to purposefully stay away from something

cause – something that brings about something else

change – the act or instance of becoming different

condition – a state of existence as determined by a set of circumstances

consider – to regard or believe, or to think carefully about something

constant – continuously occurring or recurring

continuous – uninterrupted or unending

correct – in agreement with truth or facts, or in compliance with what is generally accepted

different – not alike in nature, form, or quality

disorder – a state or condition of turmoil or confusion

disruptive – causing disorder, turmoil, or an interruption in the way something usually is done or happens

effect – something brought about by something else

enable – to provide with means or opportunity, to make possible

enliven – to make more interesting or exciting

fact – something that is consistent with objective reality and can be proven to be true

impossible – cannot exist or occur

inevitable – impossible to avoid or prevent, certain to happen

instance – a happening or occurrence of something

interrupt – to stop or cause a break in continuity

invigorating – the quality of having an enlivening or stimulating effect

live – to be alive or to reside in a particular place

occur – to happen or take place

perceive – to sense, recognize, realize, or understand

prevent – to stop something from occurring

quality – a characteristic or the essential nature of a person or thing

recur – happening or appearing repeatedly

stimulate – to encourage or cause a spurt in activity, growth, or development

think – to use one's mind to remember, ponder, imagine, plan, decide, or otherwise produce thought

turmoil – a state of great commotion, confusion, or agitation

usual – what most often happens or most often is done

CAUSE AND EFFECT

the relationship between two things in which one is the result of the other

---

SYSTEMIC CAUSATION

a causation in which interdependent events or things interact and reciprocally affect one another and sometimes transform into events or things that did not previously exist

CHAIN REACTION

a series of events in which each event causes or influences the next subsequent event

DIRECT CAUSATION

a cause and effect relationship in which no events or things intervene between the cause and effect

1. Do you think that what we choose to do now often affects which choices we have later? Why or why not?
2. Is there any action that a person can take that results only in direct causation? If so, how often do you think that happens?
3. Can you think of any action you have taken that resulted only in direct causation? If so, what were the circumstances that made this possible?

---

action – something done or accomplished

affect – to act on or cause change

causation – the relationship between cause and effect

cause – something that brings about something else

cause and effect – the relationship between two things in which one is the result of the other

chain reaction – a series of events in which each event causes or influences the next subsequent event

choices – the options from which something is selected

choose – to select after consideration

circumstance – a determining factor or set of factors

direct causation – a cause and effect relationship in which no events or things intervene between the cause and effect

effect – something brought about by something else

event – something that takes place, especially a significant occurrence

exist – to have actual being at a particular point in time

influence – a power to change a someone's belief or behavior or to affect a course of events without exerting direct control or apparent effort

interact – to act reciprocally or one upon another

interdependent – influenced or impacted by each other

intervene – to come between or interfere

later – at a subsequent time

person – an individual human being

possible – can happen or be done

previous – coming or occurring before whatever is next in time or order

produce – to bring about or create

reciprocal – an equivalent or similar action done in response to another's action

relationship – the state of being related or interrelated; a connection, association, or involvement

result – to occur as a consequence, effect, or conclusion

series – a group of objects coming one after the other

systemic causation – a causation in which interdependent events or things interact and reciprocally affect one another and sometimes transform into events or things that did not previously exist

think – to use one's mind to remember, ponder, imagine, plan, decide, or otherwise produce thought

transform – to change in appearance, composition, or structure

SELF

the total, essential, or particular being of an individual human

---

SELFLESS
having no concern for one's own advantage or well-being

SELF-INTERESTED
concerned for one's own advantage and well-being

SELF-CENTERED
concerned solely or chiefly with one's own advantage, pleasure, or well-being

SELF-AWARE
aware of oneself, including one's capabilities, traits, feelings, beliefs, and behaviors

SELF-ABSORBED

preoccupied with one's own wants and needs and not caring about the needs or feelings of others

SELF-ESTEEM

one's sense of one's own worth and value

---

1. With the possible exception of members of your family, do you believe it is realistic to expect anyone to have a greater interest than yourself in your well-being? On what do you base your belief?

2. With the possible exception of members of your family, do you believe it is realistic to expect anyone to have a greater interest in your well-being than in their own? On what do you base your belief?

3. How well do you believe that you know yourself? Is this perception of yourself fact-based?

4. How would you describe yourself in terms of being selfless vs. self-interested vs. self-centered and also in terms of being self-aware vs. self-absorbed?

5. Do you or do you not think that self-esteem must be earned? Why

6. Do you think it is possible, or even likely, that many people who present or consider themselves to be selfless and altruistic are actually primarily self-centered? Why or why not?

actual – existing in fact or reality

advantage – anything that makes doing something easier to do or more likely to happen

altruistic – concerned for the welfare of others

aware – having or showing realization or perception

behavior – the way one acts or conducts oneself

being – the fact of existence

belief – a person's conviction about the truth, existence, or validity of something

believe – to accept the truth, existence, or validity of something

capable – having the capacity and ability needed to do something

concern – the act of being attentive to or caring about something

consider – to regard or believe, or to think carefully about something

earned – acquired in exchange for work done

essential – absolutely necessary, indispensable

expect – to anticipate or think likely

family – a group of people who are biologically or legally related to one another

feeling – an emotional state or reaction

human – a person; reference to the species *homo sapiens*

individual – reference to a single human being or other single distinct entity

interest – concern about or involvement with something or someone

justifiable – having proof or sufficient reason to believe that something is right or valid

know – to perceive or understand with clarity or certainty

likely – probably will happen or is expected to happen

need – something that is required or necessary

opinion – belief about something that may or may not be based on fact or knowledge

particular – reference to a single person or thing rather than to others

pleasure – a feeling of gladness or being pleased

possible – can happen or be done

preoccupy – to dominate one's mind or attention

primary – of greatest importance or most significant

realistic – having an awareness of things as they actually are rather than as they are imagined or desired to be

reasonable – as much as is appropriate, fair, or sensible, not excessive

self – the total, essential, or particular being of an individual human

self-absorbed – preoccupied with one's own wants and needs and not caring about the needs or feelings of others

self-aware – aware of oneself, including one's capabilities, traits, feelings, beliefs, and behaviors

self-centered – concerned solely or chiefly with one's own advantage, pleasure, or well-being

self-esteem – one's sense of one's own worth and value

self-interested – concerned for one's own advantage and well-being

selfless – having no concern for one's own advantage or well-being

sense – a feeling or perception

term – a word or expression that when used contextually has precise meaning

think – to use one's mind to remember, ponder, imagine, plan, decide, or otherwise produce thought

total – the whole amount or complete scope of something

trait – a genetically determined characteristic

value – the usefulness or importance of someone or something

well-being – a satisfactory state or condition

worth – the character or intrinsic qualities of someone or something

PURPOSE

the objective toward which one strives

LEARN
to acquire knowledge or skill or to become aware and informed

UNDERSTAND
to comprehend the nature, significance, or explanation of something

MORAL
adhering to standards of responsible, respectful, and fair behavior

PRODUCTIVE
achieving or creating something of significant value

WISDOM
sound judgment based on a deep and perceptive understanding of reality

1. Do you think that having purpose in life is more closely related to identifying goals or to being useful? Why?

2. How important to you are things like continuous lifelong learning, being a moral person, living a productive life, or developing wisdom? Are there other comparable things that are equally or more important to you?

3. Specifically how do you expect to achieve things that are important to you?

---

achieve – to accomplish something important

acquire – to gain or come into ownership or possession of something

adhere – to be attached or to remain devoted

aware – having or showing realization or perception

behavior – the way one acts or conducts oneself

comparable – being enough alike to be considered generally equivalent

comprehend – to grasp or perceive the nature or meaning of something

continuous – uninterrupted or unending

create – to cause to exist or bring into being

develop – to grow into or bring to a more mature, advanced, or effective state

equal – of the same importance, quality, or amount

expect – to anticipate or think likely

fair – absence of bias, impartial

goal – the object of ambition or effort or a desired result

identify – to recognize as a particular person or thing

important – something that is necessary or that has significant worth or value

informed – the condition of being aware, knowledgeable, or educated

judgment – the ability to make considered decisions or come to sensible conclusions

knowledge – information acquired through experience, schooling, or study

learn – to acquire knowledge or skill or to become aware and informed

life – aspect of organic existence which grows and evolves

moral – adhering to standards of responsible, respectful, and fair behavior

nature – the inherent character or basic constitution of a person or thing

objective – a goal toward which effort is directed

perceptive – having or showing keen insight, understanding, or intuition

person – an individual human being

productive – achieving or creating something of significant value

provide – to make available or to supply

purpose – the objective toward which one strives

reality – the state of things as they actually are rather than as they are imagined or desired to be

relate – to have connection or reference

respectful – feeling or showing due regard and tolerance for self and others

responsible – dependable and trustworthy

significant – important and deserving of attention

skill – learned ability to do something in an efficient and capable way

sound – without defect as to truth, wisdom, or reason

specific – explicitly and clearly set forth

standard – an established or acceptable measure of value, quality, or quantity

strive – to exert significant effort to accomplish

think – to use one's mind to remember, ponder, imagine, plan, decide, or otherwise produce thought

understand – to comprehend the nature, significance, or explanation of something

understanding – the condition or quality of having the ability to comprehend and judge the nature and significance of something

useful – helpful, suited to purpose

value – the usefulness or importance of someone or something

wisdom – sound judgment based on a deep and perceptive understanding of reality

worth – the character or intrinsic qualities of someone or something

CHOICES

the options from which something is selected

MOTIVATION
the interests and concerns of a person which determine attitude and behavior

INCENTIVE
a reward offered to encourage one to do something, an extrinsic inducement that can or does incite determination or action

CONSTRAINT
a limiting or controlling condition

DELIBERATE
acting after careful and thorough thought and consideration

IMPULSIVE
acting suddenly without planning or consideration

1. Do you think it is realistic to expect people to mostly do what they believe is in their own self-interest? Why or why not?

2. Have you ever had a friend who you would allow to make important decisions for you about how you live your life? If so, who?

3. Can you identify any living person who you want to make important decisions about how you live your life? If so, who?

4. Have choices you made ever turned out to affect you or others in unexpected ways? If so, why do you think that happened?

5. Do you normally think about how choices that you make might affect others?

6. Do you think some decisions you make might be different if you made them in another time and place? Why or why not?

7. When making decisions, do you consider what both the immediate and long-term consequences of your decision might be?

8. Do you think there actually are such things as group ideas or group decisions? Why or why not?

---

act – to do something

action – something done or accomplished

actual – existing in fact or reality

affect – to act on or cause change

allow – to permit or let happen

attitude – the general way of thinking, feeling, or behaving that reflects a person's state of mind or disposition

behavior – the way one acts or conducts oneself

believe – to accept the truth, existence, or validity of something

careful – cautious in one's actions, attentive to potential danger, error, or harm

choices – the options from which something is selected

concern – the act of being attentive to or caring about something

condition – a state of existence as determined by a set of circumstances

conscious – focused on or being aware of something in particular

consequence – an effect, result, or outcome

consider – to regard or believe, or to think carefully about something

consideration – careful, deliberate thought

constraint – a limiting or controlling condition

control – to exercise authoritative power or dominating influence

decision – act of resolving a question or issue or of choosing between two or more courses of action

deliberate – acting after careful and thorough thought and consideration

determination – firm or fixed intention to accomplish a desired result

determine – to identify, establish, or decide

different – not alike in nature, form, or quality

encourage – to influence or help motivate someone to do something

expect – to anticipate or think likely

extrinsic – something originating or derived from outside itself

group – a number of similar individuals or things considered together as one

idea – a thought or opinion that is the product of mental understanding, awareness, or activity

identify – to recognize as a particular person or thing

important – something that is necessary or that has significant worth or value

impulsive – acting suddenly without planning or consideration

incentive – a reward offered to encourage one to do something, an extrinsic inducement that can or does incite determination or action

incite – to move or provoke to action

induce – to move by persuasion or influence

interest – something that arouses curiosity or draws attention

life – aspect of organic existence which grows and evolves

limit – something that bounds, restricts, or restrains

live – to be alive or to reside in a particular place

motivation – the interests and concerns of a person which determine attitude and behavior

normal – something considered to be usual or typical or without abnormalities or deficiencies

option – an alternative course of action that can be chosen from a set of possibilities

person – an individual human being

realistic – having an awareness of things as they actually are rather than as they are imagined or desired to be

self-interested – concerned for one's own advantage and well-being

think – to use one's mind to remember, ponder, imagine, plan, decide, or otherwise produce thought

thorough – exhaustively complete, without negligence or omissions

time and place – unique and virtually immeasurable number of combinations of points in time and space

unexpected – not anticipated nor thought likely

HAPPINESS

a positive state of mind, attitude, or feeling about how one is living and has lived one's life

---

SATISFACTION
feeling pleased about accomplishing a goal, meeting an expectation, or fulfilling a need

CONTENTMENT
being at ease in one's situation, without desire for change

JOY
a feeling of delight or elation

INTRINSIC
relating to the essential nature of a person or thing

EXTRINSIC

something originating or derived from outside itself

---

1. Do you think your own happiness is affected more by the aptitudes and talents with which you were born or by your success in developing and using those aptitudes and talents? Why?

2. What do you think is alike and different about the feelings of satisfaction, contentment, and joy?

3. Do you think your happiness or lack of happiness is due more than anything else to the choices that you make? Why or why not?

---

accomplish – to do something successfully

affect – to act on or cause change

aptitude – a natural capacity for learning

attitude – the general way of thinking, feeling, or behaving that reflects a person's state of mind or disposition

change – the act or instance of becoming different

choices – the options from which something is selected

contentment – being at ease in one's situation, without desire for change

derive – to take, receive, or obtain from a specific source

desire – something wanted or wished for

develop – to grow into or bring to a more mature, advanced, or effective state

different – not alike in nature, form, or quality

elation – a feeling or state of bliss or great joy

essential – absolutely necessary, indispensable

extrinsic – something originating or derived from outside itself

feeling – an emotional state or reaction

fulfill – to carry out or bring to realization

goal – the object of ambition or effort or a desired result

happiness – a positive state of mind, attitude, or feeling about how one is living and has lived one's life

intrinsic – relating to the essential nature of a person or thing

joy – a feeling of delight or elation

life – all of the experiences and actions that constitute a person's existence

live – to be alive or to reside in a particular place

nature – the inherent character or basic constitution of a person or thing

need – something that is required or necessary

originate – to come into or bring into being

person – an individual human being

positive – full of hope and confidence

principal – most important or consequential

relate – to have connection or reference

result – to occur as a consequence, effect, or conclusion

satisfaction – feeling pleased about accomplishing a goal, meeting an expectation, or fulfilling a need

situation – the circumstances and what is occurring at a particular time and place

state of mind – relating to state of a person's emotional and cognitive processes

success – favorable or desirable outcome

talent – an exceptional aptitude or ability to do something

think – to use one's mind to remember, ponder, imagine, plan, decide, or otherwise produce thought

use – to put into action or service or employ for a purpose

MORALITY

relating to or concerned with the standards of personal behavior

---

MORAL
adhering to standards of responsible, respectful, and fair behavior

RESPONSIBLE
accountable for own conduct; dependable and trustworthy

IRRESPONSIBLE
not accountable for own conduct; not dependable or trustworthy

RESPECTFUL
feeling or showing due regard and tolerance for self and others

DISRESPECTFUL
feeling or showing a lack of tolerance or civility

FAIR
absence of bias, impartial

UNFAIR
characterized by injustice, partiality, or deception

FORGIVE
to pardon an offense or offender or to eliminate consequence

---

1. Do you think there is a more correct definition of the word "moral" than "adhering to standards of responsible, respectful, and fair behavior?" If so, how do the two definitions differ?

2. Do you think there is a more correct definition of the word "respect" than "due regard and tolerance for self and others?" If so, how do these two definitions differ?

3. Why do you think some people avoid or refuse to take personal responsibility for what they do?

4. Do you think you are responsible for the actions or behavior of anyone except yourself? Why or why not?

5. Do you believe that forgiving someone for doing something harmful is respectful or fair to those who were harmed? Why or why not?

6. In your opinion, is forgiving a person who did a harmful act fair to the person who did the harmful act? Why or why not? Is it fair to society? Why or why not?

_____

absence – the condition of not being present

accountable – subject to an obligation to report, explain, or justify one's behavior

act – to do something

action – something done or accomplished

adhere – to be attached or to remain devoted

avoid – to purposefully stay away from something

behavior – the way one acts or conducts oneself

believe – to accept the truth, existence, or validity of something

bias – inclination or tendency to favor one over another

characterize – to describe the qualities or peculiarities of a person or thing

civility – the quality or act of being courteous or polite

concern – the act of being attentive to or caring about something

conduct – personal behavior, way of acting, or bearing or deportment

consequence – an effect, result, or outcome

consider – to regard or believe, or to think carefully about something

correct – in agreement with truth or facts, or in compliance with what is generally accepted

deception – act of causing someone to believe something that is misleading or hides the truth

definition – a brief explanation of the meaning of a word or phrase

dependable – consistently behaves or acts in an expected and sensible way

disrespectful – feeling or showing a lack of tolerance or civility

due – fair and proper

eliminate – to remove or omit

fair – absence of bias, impartial

feeling – an emotional state or reaction

forgive – to pardon an offense or offender or to eliminate consequence

harm – to do or cause physical or psychological damage or injury; an immoral or unjust effect

impartial – lack of preference for one thing over another

injustice – unfair, morally wrong

irresponsible – not accountable for own conduct; not dependable or trustworthy

moral – adhering to standards of responsible, respectful, and fair behavior

morality – relating to or concerned with the standards of personal behavior

offense – a violation or infraction of law or moral standard

pardon – to excuse an offense without exacting a penalty or punishment

partial – bias toward or preference for one thing over another

personal responsibility – the idea that all people should be accountable for their own decisions and actions

regard – careful consideration or attention

relate – to have connection or reference

respectful – feeling or showing due regard and tolerance for self and others

responsibility – the condition of being obligated to deal with something or being accountable for something

responsible – accountable for own conduct; dependable and trustworthy

self – the total, essential, or particular being of an individual human

society – a group of people who live as interdependent members of a community

standard – an established or acceptable measure of value, quality, or quantity

think – to use one's mind to remember, ponder, imagine, plan, decide, or otherwise produce thought

tolerance – patient indulgence with beliefs or behaviors of others that are different from one's own

trustworthy – deserving of trust or confidence

unfair – characterized by injustice, partiality, or deception

CHARACTER

moral or ethical quality

PRINCIPLES

rules or standards of action or conduct

ETHICS

one's own moral philosophy or a personal code of conduct

MORALS

a society's rules or standards for desirable or acceptable personal behavior

INTEGRITY

unwavering adherence to a moral standard or ethical code

VALUES
personal beliefs that guide individual behavior

PRINCIPLED
consistently acting in accord with one's own code of ethical conduct

VIRTUE
moral excellence

JUDGMENTAL
being quick to criticize the actions of others, often without understanding the reasons for their beliefs or behavior

---

1. Does your personal code of ethics differ from society's standards for moral behavior? If so, in what ways?

2. Do you consider it more important to be honest with yourself or to be honest with others? Which do you think is more difficult?

3. Do you think of yourself as a principled person? Why or why not?

4. What do you think are the intrinsic and extrinsic effects of being or not being a principled person?

5. Do you think a person can at the same time be both principled and judgmental? Why or why not?

acceptable – suitable to meet a need or standard

accord – to be in agreement, conformity, or harmony

act – to do something

action – something done or accomplished

adhere – to be attached or to remain devoted

behavior – the way one acts or conducts oneself

belief – a person's conviction about the truth, existence, or validity of something

character – moral or ethical quality

code – a system of principles or rules

conduct – personal behavior, way of acting, or bearing or deportment

consider – to regard or believe, or to think carefully about something

consistent – free from variation

criticize – to find fault or express disapproval of someone or something

desirable – worth wanting, doing, or achieving

difficult – hard to do or hard to deal with

effect – something brought about by something else

ethics – one's own moral philosophy or a personal code of conduct

excellent – highest or finest quality, exceptionally good

extrinsic – something originating or derived from outside itself

honest – free of deceit and untruthfulness to self and others

important – something that is necessary or that has significant worth or value

individual – reference to a single human being or other single distinct entity

integrity – unwavering adherence to a moral standard or ethical code

intrinsic – relating to the essential nature of a person or thing

judgmental – being quick to criticize the actions of others, often without understanding the reasons for their beliefs or behavior

moral – adhering to standards of responsible, respectful, and fair behavior

morals – a society's rules or standards for desirable or acceptable personal behavior

person – an individual human being

personal – anything that relates or pertains to an individual person's own self

philosophy – a system of thought

principles – rules or standards of action or conduct

principled – consistently acting in accord with one's own code of ethical conduct

reason – the basis or motive for an action, decision, or belief

rule – a standard of judgment or action

situation – the circumstances and what is occurring at a particular time and place

society – a group of people who live as interdependent members of a community

standard – an established or acceptable measure of value, quality, or quantity

think – to use one's mind to remember, ponder, imagine, plan, decide, or otherwise produce thought

time – the indefinite continuance of the past, present, and future

understanding – the condition or quality of having the ability to comprehend and judge the nature and significance of something

unwavering – characterized by firm and steady determination or resolve

values – personal beliefs that guide individual behavior

virtue – moral excellence

ATTITUDE

the general way of thinking, feeling, or behaving that reflects a person's state of mind or disposition

BEHAVIOR

the way one acts or conducts oneself

MOTIVATION
the interests and concerns of a person which determine attitude and behavior

INTELLIGENT
having or showing the capacity or ability to reason and understand

STUPID
the quality or state of not exercising or showing sound judgment

OPTIMISTIC
inclined to take a positive view of events or conditions and expect favorable outcomes

PESSIMISTIC
inclined to take a negative view of events or conditions and expect unfavorable outcomes

GULLIBLE
easily deceived, fooled, or cheated

OPEN-MINDED
willing to consider new and different ideas or the opinions of others

FANATICAL
having or showing extreme devotion to some usually social or religious ideal or goal

HUMBLE
modest in behavior and attitude; aware of inherent limitations and imperfections of human beings

ARROGANT
having or showing an exaggerated or pretentious sense of one's own importance, abilities, or understanding

PRIDE
a feeling of pleasure or satisfaction taken in an achievement, possession, or association; feeling or showing justifiable self-esteem

CONCEIT
an arrogant assumption of superiority; an excessively favorable opinion of one's own abilities, value, or worth

HUBRIS
extreme or foolish pride, conceit, or dangerous overconfidence

REASON
the basis or motive for an action, decision, or belief

EXCUSE
attempt to explain or justify what turns out to have been an ill-considered action, decision, or belief

---

1. Do you believe attitude or ability is more likely to produce personal success? On what do you base your belief?

2. Do you think that we choose to act intelligently or stupidly? Why or why not?

3. Do you think that one can often cause something to happen by expecting it to happen? Why or why not?

4. Do you or do you not consider yourself to be an open-minded person? Is your opinion about yourself fact-based?

5. Does being willing to admit that one is mistaken about something when it is embarrassing or otherwise problematic to do so seem important to you? Why or why not?

6. Do you think it is always, sometimes, or never disrespectful for us, either individually or collectively, to insist that others change their beliefs or behavior to be the same as our own? Why?

7. Do you think it is more useful to think of human behavior, both individually and collectively, in terms of virtue or evil or instead in terms of acceptable or unacceptable? Why?

---

ability – the capacity, knowledge, and skill to do something

acceptable – suitable to meet a need or standard

achieve – to accomplish something important

act – to do something

action – something done or accomplished

arrogant – having or showing an exaggerated or pretentious sense of one's own importance, abilities, or understanding

association – being involved with or connected to someone or something

attitude – the general way of thinking, feeling, or behaving that reflects a person's state of mind or disposition

aware – having or showing realization or perception

basis – something that underlies, supports, or is essential to something else

behavior – the way one acts or conducts oneself

being – a living thing

belief – a person's conviction about the truth, existence, or validity of something

believe – to accept the truth, existence, or validity of something

capacity – availability, power, or fitness to act

cause – something that brings about something else

change – the act or instance of becoming different

choose – to select after consideration

collective – some number of people acting as a group

conceit – an arrogant assumption of superiority; an excessively favorable opinion of one's own abilities, value, or worth

concern – the act of being attentive to or caring about something

condition – a state of existence as determined by a set of circumstances

conduct – personal behavior, way of acting, or bearing or deportment

consider – to regard or believe, or to think carefully about something

dangerous – involving possible injury, harm, or loss

deceive – to cause to believe something is not true or valid

decision – act of resolving a question or issue or of choosing between two or more courses of action

determine – to identify, establish, or decide

devotion – profound dedication, loyalty, or affection

different – not alike in nature, form, or quality

disposition – usual mood or attitude, inclination to think act in a particular way

disrespectful – feeling or showing a lack of tolerance or civility

event – something that takes place, especially a significant occurrence

evil – morally bad or sinful

exaggerate – to characterize something as larger, more important, better, or worse than it actually is

excessive – more than what is usual, proper, or necessary

excuse – attempt to explain or justify what turns out to have been an ill-considered action, decision, or belief

expect – to anticipate or think likely

extreme – far exceeding the ordinary or usual

fanatical – having or showing extreme devotion to some usually social or religious ideal or goal

favorable – helpful, tending to promote or facilitate

feeling – an emotional state or reaction; a mostly vague and imprecisely sourced belief

foolish – silly or unwise, having or showing a lack of common sense, good judgment, or discretion

general – concerned with, applicable to, or affecting the whole

goal – the object of ambition or effort or a desired result

gullible – easily deceived, fooled, or cheated

hubris – extreme or foolish pride, conceit, or dangerous overconfidence

human – reference to the species *homo sapiens*

humble – modest in behavior and attitude; aware of inherent limitations and imperfections of human beings

idea – a thought or opinion that is the product of mental understanding, awareness, or activity

ideal – a conception of something that in its absolute perfection exists only in the imagination or an ultimate goal or aim

ill-considered – unwise or foolish, not showing careful thought

imperfect – characterized by defects or weaknesses

important – something that is necessary or that has significant worth or value

inclination – a preference for thinking or acting in a particular way

individual – reference to a single human being or other single distinct entity

inherent – existing as something inseparable from the whole

intelligent – having or showing the capacity or ability to reason and understand

interest – something that arouses curiosity or draws attention

judgment – the ability to make considered decisions or come to sensible conclusions

justify – to show or prove that something is right or valid

likely – probably will happen or is expected to happen

limit – something that bounds, restricts, or restrains

modest – having or showing a restrained or moderate opinion of one's own capabilities or achievements

motivation – the interests and concerns of a person which determine attitude and behavior

motive – reason a person does something or considers doing something

negative – not expecting good things to happen

open-minded – willing to consider new and different ideas or the opinions of others

opinion – belief about something that may or may not be based on fact or knowledge

optimistic – inclined to take a positive view of events or conditions and expect favorable outcomes

outcome – a consequence, end result, or final product

overconfidence – excessive or unjustified trust in one's judgment or abilities

person – an individual human being

personal – anything that relates or pertains to an individual person's own self

pessimistic – inclined to take a negative view of events or conditions and expect unfavorable outcomes

pleasure – a feeling of gladness or being pleased

positive – full of hope and confidence

possess – to have under one's power or control

pride – a feeling of pleasure or satisfaction taken in an achievement, possession, or association; feeling or showing justifiable self-esteem

problematic – to cause or be full of difficulties

produce – to bring about or create

quality – a characteristic or the essential nature of a person or thing

reason – the basis or motive for an action, decision, or belief

religious – having strong belief in and reverence for a deity or deities

satisfaction – feeling pleased about accomplishing a goal, meeting an expectation, or fulfilling a need

sense – a feeling or perception

social – relating to the way people live together and interact with others

sound – without defect as to truth, wisdom, or reason

state – the whole being of something

state of mind – relating to state of a person's emotional and cognitive processes

stupid – the quality or state of not exercising or showing sound judgment

success – favorable or desirable outcome; accomplishment of something desired, planned, or attempted

think – to use one's mind to remember, ponder, imagine, plan, decide, or otherwise produce thought

thinking – the act of using one's mind to produce thought

unacceptable – not suitable to meet a need or standard

understand – to comprehend the nature, significance, or explanation of something

understanding – the condition or quality of having the ability to comprehend and judge the nature and significance of something

unfavorable – not favorable or advantageous

useful – helpful, suited to purpose

value – the usefulness or importance of someone or something

view – an opinion, belief, or idea, or a way of thinking about something

virtue – moral excellence

worth – the character or intrinsic qualities of someone or something

BALANCE

a condition of equilibrium produced by proper distribution of counteracting forces

ALIGNMENT

a favorably arranged state of mutual support

WORK
mental or physical effort expended to accomplish or produce something

PLAY
to engage in an activity for amusement or recreation

EXTROVERT
a person who is naturally inclined to maximize social engagement

INTROVERT

a person who is inclined to limit social engagement or embraces a greater than average preference for solitude

CRITICAL THINKING SKILLS

ability to gather, interpret, and objectively evaluate and analyze information as the means to solve problems, make decisions, and form judgments

INTERPERSONAL SKILLS

abilities related to the emotional or cognitive activities of an individual concerning self, specifically self-awareness of one's own talents, beliefs, values, and attitude, and the effect such awareness has on one's decisions, behavior, and point of view

PEOPLE SKILLS

ability to communicate effectively, work collaboratively, and build worthwhile relationships with others

ATHLETIC APTITUDE

capacity to perform physical activities that require agility, dexterity, strength, swiftness, or other similar qualities

MATHEMATICAL APTITUDE

capacity to understand mathematical operations, and more broadly, the capacity to analyze situations and solve problems logically

VERBAL APTITUDE

capacity to reason using concepts framed in words, crucial to abstract thinking, working memory, and written and spoken communication

VISUAL-SPATIAL APTITUDE

capacity to identify, integrate, and analyze visual forms and multidimensional spatial relationships

OCCUPATION

an activity in which one regularly engages as a means to obtain the necessities of life

VOCATION

an occupation to which one is particularly attracted

HOBBY

an activity in which one engages mainly for pleasure or relaxation

---

1. Do you think doing things that for you are difficult to do is important? Why or why not?

2. What occupations, vocations, and hobbies do you associate with athletic, mathematical, verbal, and visual-spatial aptitudes?

3. Are there things in your life that you think are currently out of balance or out of alignment? If so, what are you doing to change this situation?

ability – the capacity, knowledge, and skill to do something

abstract thinking – ability to think in terms of principles and generalizations

accomplish – to do something successfully

activity – something requiring physical or mental effort that one or many engage in doing

alignment – a favorably arranged state of mutual support

amusement – anything that pleases or entertains

analyze – to examine something in a careful and methodical way

aptitude – a natural capacity for learning

athletic aptitude – capacity to perform physical activities that require agility, dexterity, strength, swiftness, or other similar qualities

attitude – the general way of thinking, feeling, or behaving that reflects a person's state of mind or disposition

average – a standard or level that is considered to be representative or typical of the whole of something

aware – having or showing realization or perception

balance – a condition of equilibrium produced by proper distribution of counteracting forces

behavior – the way one acts or conducts oneself

belief – a person's conviction about the truth, existence, or validity of something

capacity – the potential to learn or retain knowledge; availability, power, or fitness to act

change – to alter or modify

cognitive – relating to mental activities of thinking, reasoning, or remembering

collaboratively – an effort or way in which people work together

communicate – to share information or knowledge

concept – a generalized or abstract notion or understanding of something

condition – a state of existence as determined by a set of circumstances

counteract – to reduce or remove the effect of something by bringing to bear a contrary influence

critical thinking skills – ability to gather, interpret, and objectively evaluate and analyze information as the means to solve problems, make decisions, and form judgments

crucial – vital or very significant and important

current – occurring in or existing at the present time

decision – act of resolving a question or issue or of choosing between two or more courses of action

difficult – hard to do or hard to deal with

distribute – to place or put into position

effect – something brought about by something else

effective – skilled or able to do something well

effort – a conscious exertion of energy to do something

embrace – to accept something enthusiastically

emotion – a spontaneous mental reaction experienced as a strong feeling

engage – to come together or to take part in something

equilibrium – the condition of all things influencing the stability of a person or thing being offset or cancelled out by the forces of other influences

evaluate – to determine or the quality, importance, or value of something

extrovert – a person who is naturally inclined to maximize social engagement

force – the capacity to cause change

form – to bring into existence or to shape or mold

hobby – an activity in which one engages mainly for pleasure or relaxation

identify – to recognize as a particular person or thing

important – something that is necessary or that has significant worth or value

inclination – a preference for thinking or acting in a particular way

individual – reference to a single human being or other single distinct entity

information – facts or ideas received or given

integrate – to unite or bring parts together to form a whole

interpersonal skills – abilities related to the emotional or cognitive activities of an individual concerning self, specifically self-awareness of one's own talents, beliefs, values, and attitude, and the effect such awareness has on one's decisions, behavior, and point of view

introvert – a person who is inclined to limit social engagement or embraces a greater than average preference for solitude

judgment – a decision or position arrived at by reasoning from premises or general principles

life – aspect of organic existence which grows and evolves

limit – something that bounds, restricts, or restrains

logical – relating to or in accordance with reasoning that involves correct or reliable inference

mathematical aptitude – capacity to understand mathematical operations, and more broadly, the capacity to analyze situations and solve problems logically

maximize – to increase as much as possible

means – method or way and resources used or needed to do something

memory – the mental faculty of retaining and recalling what has been experienced and learned

mental – relating to the mind

multidimensional – having two or more spatial aspects or important or prominent parts

mutual – shared in common

natural – existing in or formed by nature

necessary – needed or required

objective – the quality or condition of not being influenced by personal beliefs or feelings in considering and representing facts

occupation – an activity in which one regularly engages as a means to obtain the necessities of life

operation – the process or series of acts required to do something

particular – reference to a single person or thing rather than to others

people skills – ability to communicate effectively, work collaboratively, and build worthwhile relationships with others

person – an individual human being

physical – relating to the material structure of organic beings

play – to engage in an activity for amusement or recreation

pleasure – a feeling of gladness or being pleased

point of view – the perspective from which we view and explain something

preference – the fact of liking, wanting, or choosing one thing rather than another

problem – an issue or question to be considered, solved, or answered

produce – to bring about or create

proper – appropriate, suitable, or correct

quality – a characteristic or the essential nature of a person or thing

reason – the ability of the human mind to think, understand, and form judgments by a process of logic

recreation – physical or mental activity engaged in primarily for fun

regular – recurring at fixed or uniform intervals

relate – to have connection or reference

relationship – the state of being related or interrelated; a connection, association, or involvement

relax – to reduce in intensity, make less severe or strict

remedy – to correct or counteract

self-aware – aware of oneself, including one's capabilities, traits, feelings, beliefs, and behaviors

similar – having common but not identical characteristics

situation – a state of affairs; the circumstances and what is occurring at a particular time and place

skill – learned ability to do something in an efficient and capable way

social – relating to the way people live together and interact with others

solitude – the state or quality of being alone

solve – to find a solution, explanation, or answer to a problem or issue

spatial – relating to the relative position, area, and size of things

specific – relating to a particular person or thing

state – the whole being of something

strength – the state or quality of having physical power or capacity

support – to serve as a foundation; to provide substantiation

talent – an exceptional aptitude or ability to do something

think – to use one's mind to remember, ponder, imagine, plan, decide, or otherwise produce thought

understand – to comprehend the nature, significance, or explanation of something

values – personal beliefs that guide individual behavior

verbal aptitude – capacity to reason using concepts framed in words, crucial to abstract thinking, working memory, and written and spoken communication

visual-spatial aptitude – capacity to identify, integrate, and analyze visual forms and multidimensional spatial relationships

vocation – an occupation to which one is particularly attracted

word – a unit of language that conveys meaning

work – mental or physical effort expended to accomplish or produce something

worthwhile – sufficiently valuable to justify investment of time, effort, or interest

REALIST

a person who accepts and deals practically with things as they are and who typically thinks in terms of personal responsibility, incentives and constraints, evolved social processes, options, and relative costs

IDEALIST

someone who envisions a perfect world rather than perceiving the real one, is often naive and impractical, and typically thinks in terms of social responsibility and social justice, often with little or no consideration to logical inconsistencies, means, or costs

MOTIVATION

the interests and concerns of a person which determine attitude and behavior

INCENTIVE

a reward offered to encourage one to do something, an extrinsic inducement that can or does incite determination or action

CONSTRAINT

a limiting or controlling condition

EQUALITY

the condition or quality of all members of a society being equal, specifically as it relates to the rights and opportunities of each individual

EQUITY

the state or condition of all members of a society being treated in an equal and just way; redefined by progressives as somehow assuring exactly equal outcome for each person, regardless of personal intellect, interests, abilities, or behavior

---

1. Which do you think, realism or idealism, is more closely related to fact and fantasy? Why?

2. Who do you think is more likely to live a happy and fulfilled life, a person who generally is a realist or a person who generally is an idealist? Why?

3. Are your friends and family mostly realists or idealists?

4. Do you think of yourself as a realist or an idealist? Why?

5. In what ways do you think the notion of equity, also referred to by progressives as social justice, is affected by motivations, incentives, and constraints?

---

ability – the capacity, knowledge, and skill to do something

action – something done or accomplished

affect – to act on or cause change

assure – to make certain or cause to feel certain

attitude – the general way of thinking, feeling, or behaving that reflects a person's state of mind or disposition

behavior – the way one acts or conducts oneself

common – familiar or typical

concern – the act of being attentive to or caring about something

condition – a state of existence as determined by a set of circumstances

consideration – careful, deliberate thought

constraint – a limiting or controlling condition

control – to exercise authoritative power or dominating influence

cost – money or other resource expended to acquire, produce, or maintain something

definition – a brief explanation of the meaning of a word or phrase

determination – firm or fixed intention to accomplish a desired result

determine – to identify, establish, or decide

effect – something brought about by something else

encourage – to influence or help motivate someone to do something

envision – to conceive or see in one's mind

equal – of the same importance, quality, or amount

equality – the condition or quality of all members of a society being equal, specifically as it relates to the rights and opportunities of each individual

equity – the state or condition of all members of a society being treated in an equal and just way; redefined by progressives as somehow assuring exactly equal outcome for each person, regardless of personal intellect, interests, abilities, or behavior

evolved social processes – systemically formed social processes that adapt spontaneously to the needs of society

extrinsic – something originating or derived from outside itself

fact – something that is consistent with objective reality and can be proven to be true

family – a group of people who are biologically or legally related to one another

fantasy – something that is created by and exists only in the imagination

fulfill – to carry out or bring to realization

general – concerned with, applicable to, or affecting the whole

happy – feeling satisfaction, contentment, and joy

idealist – someone who envisions a perfect world rather than perceiving the real one, is often naive and impractical, and typically thinks in terms of social responsibility and social justice, often with little or no consideration to logical inconsistencies, means, or cost

impractical – not practical or useful

incentive – a reward offered to encourage one to do something, an extrinsic inducement that can or does incite determination or action

incite – to move or provoke to action

individual – reference to a single human being or other single distinct entity

induce – to move by persuasion or influence

intellect – a person's capacity for learning, thinking, and understanding

interest – concern about or involvement with something or someone; something that arouses curiosity or draws attention

just – conforming to a standard of fair treatment and due reward

life – aspect of organic existence which grows and evolves; all of the experiences and actions that constitute a person's existence

likely – probably will happen or is expected to happen

limit – something that bounds, restricts, or restrains

logical – relating to or in accordance with reasoning that involves correct or reliable inference

logically inconsistent – a set of assertions, ideas, statements, or the like that cannot all be true at the same time; an unresolvable contradiction between parts of an argument

means – method or way and resources used or needed to do something

motivation – the interests and concerns of a person which determine attitude and behavior

naive – lacking knowledge, comprehension, or concern; unaware or unsuspecting

notion – vague or imprecise impression or idea

opportunity – a situation which makes it possible to do something in particular

option – an alternative course of action that can be chosen from a set of possibilities

outcome – a consequence, end result, or final product

perceive – to sense, recognize, realize, or understand

perfect – the unattainable state or condition of being without any fault or defect

person – an individual human being

personal – anything that relates or pertains to an individual person's own self

personal responsibility – the idea that all people should be accountable for their own decisions and actions

practical – concerned with the actual doing of something or in fact being useful rather than with theory and ideas

progressive – one who believes in enforcing social equality through vigorous governmental action

quality – a characteristic or the essential nature of a person or thing; level of excellence

realist – a person who accepts and deals practically with things as they are and who typically thinks in terms of personal responsibility, incentives and constraints, social processes, options, and relative costs

relate – to have connection or reference

relative – considered in comparison or relation to something else

rights – entitlements to which each person has an equal moral or legal claim

social – relating to the way people live together and interact with others

social justice – a socially progressive concept of fair and just relations between the individual and society that commits to providing to all equal wealth, opportunities for personal activity, and social privileges

social responsibility – socially progressive idea that all people who have an ability to affect change that they believe is beneficial to society also have an obligation to make use of that ability however they can

society – a group of people who live as interdependent members of a community

specific – relating to a particular person or thing

state – the whole being of something

term – a word or expression that when used contextually has precise meaning

think – to use one's mind to remember, ponder, imagine, plan, decide, or otherwise produce thought

tradition – time-honored institutions and established customs

treat – to deal with something or someone in a particular way

typical – the generally common characteristics or behavior of a group of people or things

word – a unit of language that conveys meaning

world – the earthly state of human existence

WORTH

the character or intrinsic qualities of someone or something

VALUE

the usefulness or importance of someone or something

MORAL
adhering to standards of responsible, respectful, and fair behavior

PRODUCTIVE
achieving or creating something of significant value

VIRTUE
moral excellence; an admirable quality or trait

MERIT

demonstrated value, ability, or achievement

---

1. Do you think a person's worth and value are interrelated? If so, how?

2. What criteria do you generally use to assess the worth of a person? Do you use the same criteria to assess the worth of a person in every situation? Why or why not?

3. What criteria do you generally use to assess the value of a person? Do you use the same criteria to assess the value of a person in every situation? Why or why not?

4. Do you think the criteria others typically use to assess the worth and value of people are different from your own? If so, in what ways?

5. Why do you think the value you attribute to things that you do or create is sometimes more or less than the value that others attribute to them?

---

ability – the capacity, knowledge, and skill to do something

achieve – to accomplish something important

adhere – to be attached or to remain devoted

assessment – the action or product of determining the value, significance, or extent of something

attribute – to regard as a quality, characteristic, or measure of a person or thing

behavior – the way one acts or conducts oneself

character – moral or ethical quality

create – to cause to exist or bring into being

criteria – the rules or ideals by which something is judged or assessed

demonstrate – to make evident or show clearly

dependent – determined or decided by someone or something else

different – not alike in nature, form, or quality

excellent – highest or finest quality, exceptionally good

fair – absence of bias, impartial

general – concerned with, applicable to, or affecting the whole

important – something that is necessary or that has significant worth or value

interrelated – the condition of things having reciprocal connections with one another

moral – adhering to standards of responsible, respectful, and fair behavior

person – an individual human being

productive – achieving or creating something of significant value

respectful – feeling or showing due regard and tolerance for self and others

responsible – accountable for own conduct; dependable and trustworthy

significant – important and deserving of attention

situation – the circumstances and what is occurring at a particular time and place

standard – an established or acceptable measure of value, quality, or quantity

think – to use one's mind to remember, ponder, imagine, plan, decide, or otherwise produce thought

use – to put into action or service or employ for a purpose

useful – helpful, suited to purpose

value – the usefulness or importance of someone or something

virtue – moral excellence; an admirable quality or trait

worth – the character or intrinsic qualities of someone or something

SOCIETY

a system of human organization that supplies protection, continuity, security, and identity; a group of people who live as interdependent members of a community

---

SOCIAL PROCESSES

the ways in which individuals and groups typically interact and form social relationships

DESIGNED SOCIAL PROCESSES

social processes that are formed and arbitrarily imposed on society by a ruling class

EVOLVED SOCIAL PROCESSES

systemically formed social processes that adapt spontaneously to the needs of society

SYSTEMIC RATIONALITY

the idea that knowledge and reasons that are unknowable to any individual participant spontaneously produce through systemic interaction reasonable decisions and outcomes for the whole

STANDARD OF LIVING

the level of material comfort experienced by a person or group of people

QUALITY OF LIFE

a subjective assessment of overall enjoyment of life

SYSTEMIC

relating to the inherent interdependencies of a system

INSTITUTIONAL

relating to or affecting an entire organization or culture, or fundamental to a social, economic, or political practice

---

1. Would you prefer to live in a society that is structured around designed social processes or evolved social processes? Why?

2. To what extent and in what ways do you think that the decisions and behavior of those in positions of political power affect your standard of living and your quality of life?

3. To what extent and in what ways do you think that the decisions and behavior of other members of society affect your standard of living and your quality of life?

4. In what ways do you think members of society should be interdependent and in what ways should they be independent?

5. Do you think the relative levels of social, economic, and political interdependence and independence that you favor would produce the highest standard of living for society as a whole? Why?

6. Do you or do you not think the word "systemic" is sometimes used when the word "institutional" or "systematic" would be more correct? If so, why do you think this occurs?

---

adapt – to make fit for a particular situation or use

affect – to act on or cause change

arbitrary – unrestrained and autocratic in the use of authority or power

assessment – the action or product of determining the value, significance, or extent of something

behavior – the way one acts or conducts oneself

comfort – the condition or cause of feeling pleasurable ease or relief

community – a group of people who live in a particular geographical area or who share common interests or points of view

continuity – uninterrupted extension in space, time, or sequence

correct – in agreement with truth or facts, or in compliance with what is generally accepted

culture – shared pattern of behavior and understanding that is learned through socialization

decision – act of resolving a question or issue or of choosing between two or more courses of action

designed social processes – social processes that are formed and arbitrarily imposed on society by a ruling class

economic – relating to production, distribution, and consumption of goods and services

evolved social processes – systemically formed social processes that adapt spontaneously to the needs of society

experience – doing, seeing, or feeling something

extent – the range, distance, space, or magnitude of something

favor – to treat with preference or partiality

form – to bring into existence or to shape or mold

fundamental – forming or serving as an essential component of a concept, system, or structure

group – a number of similar individuals or things considered together as one

human – reference to the species *homo sapiens*

idea – a thought or opinion that is the product of mental understanding, awareness, or activity

identity – the distinguishing beliefs, characteristics, or qualities of a person or group of people

impose – to force on another or others

independent – free from dominance or control of others, relying on one's own judgment, capabilities, or resources

individual – reference to a single human being or other single distinct entity

inherent – existing as something inseparable from the whole

institutional – relating to or affecting an entire organization or culture, or fundamental to a social, economic, or political practice

interact – to act reciprocally or one upon another

interaction – mutual or reciprocal action or influence

interdependent – influenced or impacted by each other

knowledge – information acquired through experience, schooling, or study

life – all of the experiences and actions that constitute a person's existence

live – to be alive or to reside in a particular place

material – having importance or consequence

need – something that is required or necessary

occur – to happen or take place

organization – a group of people who work together in a structured way for a particular purpose

outcome – a consequence, end result, or final product

overall – in general rather than in particular

participant – a person who becomes involved or takes part in something

person – an individual human being

political – relating to public affairs and governance

position – one's role and importance in an organization or in society

power – having the ability to control people or things

practice – something done regularly or constantly

produce – to bring about or create

quality of life – a subjective assessment of overall enjoyment of life

rational – relating to or involving reason or knowledge

reason – the basis or motive for an action, decision, or belief

reasonable – as much as is appropriate, fair, or sensible, not excessive

relate – to have connection or reference

relationship – the state of being related or interrelated; a connection, association, or involvement

relative – considered in comparison or relation to something else

ruling class – relatively small group of people who decide upon a society's political structure and agenda

security – free from actual risk or danger

social – relating to the way people live together and interact with others

social processes – the ways in which individuals and groups typically interact and form social relationships

society – a system of human organization that supplies protection, continuity, security, and identity; a group of people who live as interdependent members of a community

spontaneous – happening or arising without apparent external cause

standard of living – the level of material comfort experienced by a person or group of people

structure – the way parts are put together to form a whole

subjective – influenced by or based on beliefs and feelings

supply – to provide or make available

system – interacting, interrelated, or interdependent elements that form or function as a whole

systematic – methodical, characterized by thoroughness and regularity

systemic – relating to the inherent interdependencies of a system

systemic rationality – the idea that knowledge and reasons that are unknowable to any individual participant spontaneously produce through systemic interaction reasonable decisions and outcomes for the whole

think – to use one's mind to remember, ponder, imagine, plan, decide, or otherwise produce thought

typical – the generally common characteristics or behavior of a group of people or things

unknowable – impossible to know, existing beyond the capacities of human cognition or knowledge

use – to put into action or service or employ for a purpose

whole – all aspects of a thing, something in its entirety

word – a unit of language that conveys meaning

SOCIAL ORDER

a system of institutions, structures, and organizing principles that are used to maintain society

---

TRIBALISM

a sociopolitical organization that is united by ties of common ancestry, customs, and traditions

FEUDALISM

a political, social, and economic system in which people in the lower social classes are awarded limited property rights by people of higher rank and in return work and fight for their supposed benefactors

SOCIALISM

a political and social philosophy based originally on the principles of collectivism that has now morphed into an authoritarian political system that characteristically exercises tight control over political, social, and economic affairs

REPUBLICANISM
a representative form of government in which the civil liberties that are guaranteed to every citizen are codified in a constitution

MORAL
adhering to standards of responsible, respectful, and fair behavior

STANDARD OF LIVING
the level of material comfort experienced by a person or group of people

RIGHTS
entitlements to which each person has an equal moral or legal claim

PARASITIC
existing at the expense of others, often causing great harm and contributing nothing of value in return

---

1. Which social order, tribalism, feudalism, socialism, or republicanism, do you favor over all others? Why?

2. Do you think the social order that you favor is more or less moral than all others? In what ways?

3. Do you think the social order that you favor produces a higher overall standard of living than all others? Why?

4. What do you think are the principal differences between feudalism and socialism?

5. Do you think a person's rights can rightfully be infringed upon or violated? Why or why not?

6. Do you think the views or special interests of any person or group of people should take precedence over the views or interests of other members of society? Why or why not?

7. To what extent do you think parasitic behavior can be tolerated within a generally moral society? Why?

---

adhere – to be attached or to remain devoted

affair – something done or experienced; a matter of commercial, professional, public, or personal interest or concern

ancestor – a person from whom one is descended

authoritarian – favoring or enforcing strict obedience to those in positions of power

award – to grant or bestow as being merited, deserved, or needed

behavior – the way one acts or conducts oneself

benefactor – one who confers a benefit on another

cause – something that brings about something else

characteristic – a distinguishing or distinctive feature

citizen – a person who due to birth or naturalization has a specific legal relationship with a state or nation

civil liberties – individual rights that governments commit not to abridge either by legislation or judicial interpretation

codify – to establish or recognize individual rights, statutes, rules, or regulations

collectivism – belief that the priorities of a group, somehow decided, should be favored over the dignity and welfare of the individual

comfort – the condition or cause of feeling pleasurable ease or relief

common – belonging to or shared by members of a community

constitution – a written instrument embodying the rules of a political or social organization

control – to exercise authoritative power or dominating influence

custom – a long-standing and common way of doing something

different – not alike in nature, form, or quality

economic – relating to production, distribution, and consumption of goods and services

exercise – to act or bring into play

exist – to have actual being at a particular point in time

experience – doing, seeing, or feeling something

extent – the range, distance, space, or magnitude of something

fair – absence of bias, impartial

favor – to treat with preference or partiality

feudalism – a political, social, and economic system in which people in the lower social classes are awarded limited property rights by people of higher rank and in return work and fight for their supposed benefactors

form – the shape or structure of something

formal – official or proper form or structure

general – concerned with, applicable to, or affecting the whole

government – the set of formal legal institutions that are formed to administer and manage the affairs of a nation or other political community

group – a number of similar individuals or things considered together as one

guarantee – a promise or assurance of specific performance, quality, or benefit

harm – to do or cause physical or psychological damage or injury

immoral – not in accord with moral standards

individual – reference to a single human being or other single distinct entity

infringe – to encroach upon or breach the boundary of something

institution – a significant and established organization

interest – concern about or involvement with something or someone

leadership – the ability to influence and guide others toward achieving a common objective

limit – something that bounds, restricts, or restrains

material – having importance or consequence

moral – adhering to standards of responsible, respectful, and fair behavior

morph – to change or transform over time from one thing to another

organization – a group of people who work together in a structured way for a particular purpose; spontaneous or deliberate formation of arrangement or order

overall – in general rather than in particular

parasitic – existing at the expense of others, often causing great harm and contributing nothing of value in return

permanent – lasting or remaining without change

person – an individual human being

philosophy – a system of thought

political – relating to public affairs and governance

precedence – the condition of having higher priority

principal – most important or consequential

principle – a fundamental truth that serves as a foundational tenet of a system of beliefs or a chain of reasoning

produce – to bring about or create

property rights – legal protections that enable people and legal entities to own, use, and receive benefits from tangible and intangible resources and economic goods

rank – the relative position or status of a person or thing

representative – a system of governance in which members of a governmental body, usually legislative, are chosen by popular vote to make laws that advance the common interests of their constituents

republicanism – a representative form of government in which the civil liberties that are guaranteed to every citizen are codified in a constitution

respectful – feeling or showing due regard and tolerance for self and others

responsible – accountable for own conduct; dependable and trustworthy

right – conforms with ethical and moral principles

rights – entitlements to which each person has an equal moral or legal claim

social – relating to the way people live together and interact with others

social class – a group of people of similar status, rank, or common characteristics within a society who possess the same socioeconomic status

social order – the system of institutions, structures, and organizing principles that are used to maintain society

social philosophy – view of how personal and societal responsibilities and rights should be prioritized

socialism – a political and social philosophy based originally on the principles of collectivism that has now morphed into an authoritarian political system that characteristically exercises tight control over political, social, and economic affairs

society – a system of human organization that supplies protection, continuity, security, and identity

sociopolitical – relating to or involving both social and political factors

special – exceptional, surpassing what is common or usual

standard – an established or acceptable measure of value, quality, or quantity

standard of living – the level of material comfort experienced by a person or group of people

structure – the composition of something that is made from parts

system – interacting, interrelated, or interdependent elements that form or function as a whole

think – to use one's mind to remember, ponder, imagine, plan, decide, or otherwise produce thought

tolerate – to permit something to exist without prohibition or interference

tradition – time-honored institutions and established customs

tribalism – a sociopolitical organization that is united by ties of common ancestry, customs, and traditions

use – to put into action or service or employ for a purpose

value – the usefulness or importance of someone or something

view – an opinion, belief, or idea, or a way of thinking about something

violate – to act in a manner that is unlawful or immoral

work – mental or physical effort expended to accomplish or produce something

CULTURE

a shared pattern of behavior and understanding that is learned through socialization

———————————

SOCIETY
a system of human organization that supplies protection, continuity, security, and identity; a group of people who live as interdependent members of a community

DIVERSITY
the quality or condition of being different

ASSIMILATION
the act or process of absorbing and incorporating into the whole

INDEPENDENT
free from dominance or control of others; the quality of relying on one's own judgment, capabilities, or resources

INTERDEPENDENT
influenced or impacted by each other

DEPENDENT
determined or decided by someone or something else;
the quality of relying on the judgment, capabilities, or resources of others

TRUST
confident reliance on character, ability, strength, or integrity

---

1. In what ways do you think culture affects a person's beliefs and behavior?

2. In what ways and by what measure do you think cultural diversity and assimilation can best serve our society? In what ways do you think cultural diversity can be detrimental to social unity?

3. Do you think our society is best served by promoting a shared culture of personal independence or a culture of personal dependence? Why?

4. Do you or do you not think our society is best served by promoting a shared culture of trust? Why?

5. What do you think is required for a person to develop trust in oneself and in others?

---

ability – the capacity, knowledge, and skill to do something

assimilation – the act or process of absorbing and incorporating into the whole

available – accessible and ready for use

behavior – the way one acts or conducts oneself

belief – a person's conviction about the truth, existence, or validity of something

capable – having the capacity and ability needed to do something

character – moral or ethical quality

condition – a state of existence as determined by a set of circumstances

confident – certain or self-assured

consider – to regard or believe, or to think carefully about something

continuity – uninterrupted extension in space, time, or sequence

control – to exercise authoritative power or dominating influence

culture – shared pattern of behavior and understanding that is learned through socialization

current – occurring in or existing at the present time

decision – act of resolving a question or issue or of choosing between two or more courses of action

dependent – determined or decided by someone or something else; the quality of relying on the judgment, capabilities, or resources of others

determine – to identify, establish, or decide

develop – to grow into or bring to a more mature, advanced, or effective state

different – not alike in nature, form, or quality

diversity – the quality or condition of being different

dominant – commanding, controlling, or prevailing over all others

free – without restraint or restriction

group – a number of similar individuals or things considered together as one

human – reference to the species *homo sapiens*

identity – the distinguishing beliefs, characteristics, or qualities of a person or group of people

impact – to have direct effect

important – something that is necessary or that has significant worth or value

independent – free from dominance or control of others, relying on one's own judgment, capabilities, or resources

influence – a power to change a someone's belief or behavior or to affect a course of events without exerting direct control or apparent effort

integrity – unwavering adherence to a moral standard or ethical code

interdependent – influenced or impacted by each other

judgment – the ability to make considered decisions or come to sensible conclusions

learn – to acquire knowledge or skill or to become aware and informed

likely – probably will happen or is expected to happen

measure – an adequate or suitable proportion or amount

organization – a group of people who work together in a structured way for a particular purpose

pattern – an arrangement or sequence that repeats in a predictable way

person – an individual human being

personal – anything that relates or pertains to an individual person's own self

process – a series of actions or changes

promote – to help or encourage to exist or flourish

protect – to defend or shield against injury, harm, or loss

quality – a characteristic or the essential nature of a person or thing

rely – to depend on or place trust in

required – stipulated as absolutely indispensable

resource – something that has utility or that is available for use

security – free from actual risk or danger

social – relating to the way people live together and interact with others

socialization – the process of acquiring the values, habits, and attitudes of a society

society – a system of human organization that supplies protection, continuity, security, and identity; a group of people who live as interdependent members of a community

state of mind – relating to state of a person's emotional and cognitive processes

strength – the state or quality of having physical power or capacity

supply – to provide or make available

think – to use one's mind to remember, ponder, imagine, plan, decide, or otherwise produce thought

trust – confident reliance on character, ability, strength, or integrity

understanding – the condition or quality of having the ability to comprehend and judge the nature and significance of something

unity – a state or condition of oneness or standing together; being in agreement or in accord

whole – all aspects of a thing, something in its entirety

INDIVIDUALISM

belief that individual freedom and the virtues of self-reliance and personal independence should be favored over collective or state control

COLLECTIVISM

belief that the priorities of a group, somehow decided, should be favored over the dignity and welfare of the individual

———————————————

LEADER
one who shows the way and persuades others to follow

RULER
one who exercises controlling power over others

INDEPENDENCE OF MIND

the state of mind of people whose thinking and behavior are guided by their own attitudes, values, and beliefs

GROUPTHINK

the phenomenon of being influenced by peers to adopt uninformed or illogical opinions and behaviors that are common within a community to which one is connected

---

1. Do you think leaders or rulers are most likely to emerge in a society that mostly favors individualism and that mostly favors collectivism? Why?

2. Do you think economic and social innovation is more likely to occur in a society that mostly favors individualism or that mostly favors collectivism? Why?

3. What do you think a person's principal motivations might be to adopt groupthink points of view and behavior? Why?

---

adopt – to voluntarily choose to accept, follow, or take into a relationship

attitude – the general way of thinking, feeling, or behaving that reflects a person's state of mind or disposition

behavior – the way one acts or conducts oneself

belief – a person's conviction about the truth, existence, or validity of something

collective – some number of people acting as a group

collectivism – belief that the priorities of a group, somehow decided, should be favored over the dignity and welfare of the individual

common – belonging to or shared by members of a group

community – a group of people who live in a particular geographical area or who share common interests or points of view

control – to exercise authoritative power or dominating influence

decision – act of resolving a question or issue or of choosing between two or more courses of action

dignity – the worth and value of a person

economic – relating to production, distribution, and consumption of goods and services

exercise – to act or bring into play

favor – to treat with preference or partiality

freedom – the unhindered right to think, speak, and act however one wants

group – a number of similar individuals or things considered together as one

groupthink – the phenomenon of being influenced by peers to adopt uninformed or illogical opinions and behaviors that are common within a community to which one is connected

illogical – contradicting or disregarding the principles of logic

independence of mind – the state of mind of people whose thinking and behavior are guided by their own attitudes, values, and beliefs

independent – free from dominance or control of others, relying on one's own judgment, capabilities, or resources

individual – reference to a single human being or other single distinct entity

individualism – belief that individual freedom and the virtues of self-reliance and personal independence should be favored over collective or state control

influence – a power to change a someone's belief or behavior or to affect a course of events without exerting direct control or apparent effort

innovation – change that creates a new dimension of performance

leader – one who shows the way and persuades others to follow

likely – probably will happen or is expected to happen

motivation – the interests and concerns of a person which determine attitude and behavior

occur – to happen or take place

opinion – belief about something that may or may not be based on fact or knowledge

peer – person who has equal standing

person – an individual human being

personal – anything that relates or pertains to an individual person's own self

persuade – to convince someone to accept a point of view or to act by means of example, explanation, discussion, or debate

phenomenon – an observable fact or event

point of view – the perspective from which we view and explain something

power – having the ability to control people or things

principal – most important or consequential

priority – the state or fact of being more important; the relative position assigned to something

ruler – one who exercises controlling power over others

similar – having common but not identical characteristics

social – relating to the way people live together and interact with others

society – a system of human organization that supplies protection, continuity, security, and identity

state – a politically organized body of people

state of mind – relating to state of a person's emotional and cognitive processes

think – to use one's mind to remember, ponder, imagine, plan, decide, or otherwise produce thought

typical – the generally common characteristics or behavior of a group of people or things

values – personal beliefs that guide individual behavior

virtue – conformity to a standard of right; an admirable quality or trait

welfare – physical and mental health and happiness

POWER

having the ability to control people or things

CONTROL

to exercise authoritative power or dominating influence

SECURITY
free from actual risk or danger

RULE OF MAN
principle of governance that prescribed government action be based on circumstances of situation as decided arbitrarily by ruling authority

RULE OF LAW

principle of governance that restricts the arbitrary exercise of governmental control by subordinating it to well-defined and established laws under which all people are treated equally

TWO-TIERED JUSTICE

refers to a judicial system in which some people are granted greater legal immunity or are judged more leniently than others

---

1. For whom and to what extent do you think power and control produce actual security? Why?

2. What are three good reasons to rely on and three good reasons to not rely on people who consistently demonstrate they want more than anything else to exercise controlling power over others?

3. Does it or does it not seem to you that some people do whatever they can to disrupt and fracture society? If this does seem to you to be the situation, what do you think the motivations or incentives are for them to do what they do?

4. Do you think your own quality of life is better or worse when political power and control in our society is concentrated or instead is distributed and diffused? Why?

5. What effect do you think two-tiered justice has on society? Why?

ability – the capacity, knowledge, and skill to do something

action – something done or accomplished

actual – existing in fact or reality

apply – to put something to use or to put one thing on top of another

arbitrary – unrestrained and autocratic in the use of authority or power

authority – power or right to direct, control, or command; a person or group of people that has the power or right to direct, control, or command

balance – a condition of equilibrium produced by proper distribution of counteracting forces

circumstance – a determining factor or set of factors

concentrated – collected together in a single place

consistent – free from variation

control – to exercise authoritative power or dominating influence

demonstrate – to make evident or show clearly

diffuse – to weaken or make less intense

disruptive – causing disorder, turmoil, or an interruption in the way something usually is done or happens

distribute – to allocate to several or many

dominant – commanding, controlling, or prevailing over all others

effect – something brought about by something else

equal – of the same importance, quality, or amount

established – long recognized and widely accepted

exercise – to act or bring into play

extent – the range, distance, space, or magnitude of something

fracture – to divide or to damage or destroy

free – without restraint or restriction

good – satisfactory as to quality, quantity, or degree

governance – the act or process of governing or overseeing the control and direction of a society or an organization

government – the set of formal legal institutions that are formed to administer and manage the affairs of a nation or other political community

grant – to bestow, confer, or allow

immunity – circumstance of being protected from typical consequence

incentive – a reward offered to encourage one to do something, an extrinsic inducement that can or does incite determination or action

influence – a power to change a someone's belief or behavior or to affect a course of events without exerting direct control or apparent effort

judge – to consider or decide a legal matter or consequence

judicial – pertaining to courts of law or administration of justice

legal – relating to or concerned with law; established or recognized by law

lenient – merciful, not harsh or severe

motivation – the interests and concerns of a person which determine attitude and behavior

political – relating to public affairs and governance

power – having the ability to control people or things

prescribe – to mandate as a rule or course of action to be followed

principle – a fundamental truth that serves as a foundational tenet of a system of beliefs or a chain of reasoning

produce – to bring about or create

quality of life – a subjective assessment of overall enjoyment of life

reason – the basis or motive for an action, decision, or belief

rely – to depend on or place trust in

restrict – to keep within specified boundaries

risk – the condition of potentially suffering harm or loss

rule – the exercise of authority or control

rule of law – principle of governance that restricts the arbitrary exercise of governmental control by subordinating it to well-defined and established laws under which all people are treated equally

rule of man – principle of governance that prescribed government action be based on circumstances of situation as decided arbitrarily by ruling authority

security – free from actual risk or danger

situation – a state of affairs; the circumstances and what is occurring at a particular time and place

society – a system of human organization that supplies protection, continuity, security, and identity

subordinate – subject to the authority of another

system – interacting, interrelated, or interdependent elements that form or function as a whole

think – to use one's mind to remember, ponder, imagine, plan, decide, or otherwise produce thought

treat – to deal with something or someone in a particular way

two-tiered justice – refers to a judicial system in which some people are granted greater legal immunity or are judged more leniently than others

well-defined – clearly and unambiguously stated

AUTHORITARIANISM

a system in which a single person or a small group of
people possess mostly unlimited control or influence

———————————————

GOVERNMENT

the set of formal legal institutions that are formed to administer and manage
the affairs of a nation or other political community

RELIGION

faith-based organizations or institutions structured around common beliefs in
and reverence for a supernatural power or powers

ACADEMIA

the community and culture of those engaged in higher education
teaching and research

MASS MEDIA

the microcosm of journalists and advertising professionals, and entertainment, professional sports, and media celebrities

MULTINATIONAL BUSINESS ENTERPRISES

companies with substantial business operations spread across different countries

LABOR UNIONS

organizations that represent the collective interests of union members, often with legally protected and government-promoted monopolistic power

CULTS

social groups defined by their religious, spiritual, political, or philosophical beliefs, or by common interest in a particular personality, object, or unachievable goal

---

1. What effect do you think authoritarianism has on innovation and productivity in any group of people?
2. Why do you think some people seek power to rule over others?
3. Why do you think people sometimes are amenable to authoritarian rule?
4. Is there a public figure or someone you know personally that you consider to be authoritarian? If so, do you consider this person's behavior to be primarily selfless, self-interested, or self-centered? Why?

academia – the community and culture of those engaged in higher education teaching and research

administer – to direct or oversee the operation of something

advertising – promoting or creating awareness about a product, service, or cause

affair – something done or experienced; a matter of commercial, professional, public, or personal interest or concern

amenable – willing to submit to authority

authoritarian – favoring or enforcing strict obedience to those in positions of power

authoritarianism – a system in which a single person or a small group of people possess mostly unlimited control or influence

behavior – the way one acts or conducts oneself

belief – a person's conviction about the truth, existence, or validity of something

business – the activity of buying and selling commodities, products, or services

celebrity – a famous or well-known person

collective – some number of people acting as a group

common – belonging to or shared by members of a group

community – a group of people who live in a particular geographical area or who share common interests or points of view

company – a business that produces or sells goods or services

control – to exercise authoritative power or dominating influence

cults – social groups defined by their religious, spiritual, political, or philosophical beliefs, or by common interest in a particular personality, object, or unachievable goal

culture – shared pattern of behavior and understanding that is learned through socialization

different – not alike in nature, form, or quality

education – the action or process of teaching and learning; the knowledge, skills, values, beliefs, and habits learned from observation, study, and experience

effect – something brought about by something else

engage – to come together or to take part in something

faith – unwavering or unshakeable belief without proof or evidence

form – to bring into existence or to shape or mold

formal – official or proper form or structure

goal – the object of ambition or effort or a desired result

government – the set of formal legal institutions that are formed to administer and manage the affairs of a nation or other political community

group – a number of similar individuals or things considered together as one

influence – a power to change a someone's belief or behavior or to affect a course of events without exerting direct control or apparent effort

innovation – change that creates a new dimension of performance

institution – a significant and established organization

journalist – a person engaged in collecting, writing, editing, and presenting news or news articles

know – to be familiar with or have knowledge of

labor unions – organizations that represent the collective interests of union members, often with legally protected and government-promoted monopolistic power

legal – relating to or concerned with law; established or recognized by law

mass media – the microcosm of journalists and advertising professionals, and entertainment, professional sports, and media celebrities

media – members of the mass media

microcosm – a small community or society

monopoly – enterprise that is able, at least in the short term, to cause economic results different from what would otherwise occur in a free market by dominating the market for goods and services it produces or delivers

multinational business enterprises – companies with substantial business operations spread across different countries

nation – a territorially bounded sovereign political entity ruled in the name of a community of citizens who identify themselves as an independent country

object – the focus of attention, feeling, thought, or action

operation – some form of work or production

organization – a group of people who work together in a structured way for a particular purpose

particular – reference to a single person or thing rather than to others

person – an individual human being

personal – anything that relates or pertains to an individual person's own self

personality – the qualities and traits that are peculiar to a particular human or non-human animal

philosophy – the study of human values and knowledge; a system of thought

political – relating to public affairs and governance

possess – to have under one's power or control

power – being able to do what one wants; having the ability to control people or things; force required to produce an effect

primary – of greatest importance or most significant

productivity – the quality, state, or fact of being able to create, enhance, or provide goods and services

professional – engaged in an activity as an occupation

promote – to help or encourage to exist or flourish

protect – to defend or shield against injury, harm, or loss

religion – faith-based organizations or institutions structured around common beliefs in and reverence for a supernatural power or powers

religious – having strong belief in and reverence for a deity or deities

reverence – a feeling or attitude of awe and deep respect

rule – the exercise of authority or control

seek – to strive to obtain

self-centered – concerned solely or chiefly with one's own advantage, pleasure, or well-being

self-interested – concerned for one's own advantage and well-being

selfless – having no concern for one's own advantage or well-being

set – a group of similar or related things

social – relating to the way people live together and interact with others

spiritual – feeling, sense, or belief the world is affected by something that is cosmic or divine

structure – the way parts are put together to form a whole

supernatural – relating to existence outside the natural world

system – interacting, interrelated, or interdependent elements that form or function as a whole

think – to use one's mind to remember, ponder, imagine, plan, decide, or otherwise produce thought

unachievable – impossible to achieve

unlimited – having no restrictions or boundaries

HONORABLE

having or showing strict adherence to what is morally right and lawful

CORRUPT

unlawful, improper, or immoral in character or conduct

DECEIT

speech or behavior that purposefully deceives or misleads others through lies or trickery

COLLUSION

cooperation for an illegal or deceitful purpose

INSIDER TRADING
the act of basing personal investment decisions on confidential or privileged information

BRIBERY
the act of giving or taking a bribe

INFLUENCE PEDDLING
use of existing or potential influence on someone's behalf in exchange for money or favors

CRONYISM
the practice of showing partiality to friends or allies

POLITICAL PATRONAGE
appointment or hiring of someone on the basis of partisan loyalty to fill a government position

---

1. Do you think lawful behavior is sometimes also morally wrong? If so, how do you think this happens?

2. Do you think it is generally more realistic to expect people in positions of authoritarian power to be honorable or corrupt? Why?

3. Do you think corruption in our political and social institutions has or could have a significant effect on the long-term success and well-being of our society? Why or why not?

4. Do you think corruption in our political and social institutions has or could have a negative impact on your personal success? Why or why not?

_____

act – to do something

adhere – to be attached or to remain devoted

appoint – to assign to an office or position

authoritarian – favoring or enforcing strict obedience to those in positions of power

basis – something that underlies, supports, or is essential to something else

behavior – the way one acts or conducts oneself

believe – to accept the truth, existence, or validity of something

bribe – money or favor given or received to secure preferential treatment

bribery – the act of giving or taking a bribe

character – moral or ethical quality

collusion – cooperation for an illegal or deceitful purpose

conduct – personal behavior, way of acting, or bearing or deportment

confidential – strictly private or secret

cooperation – willingly working with others or acting together for a common purpose or benefit

corrupt – unlawful, improper, or immoral in character or conduct

cronyism – the practice of showing partiality to friends or allies

deceit – speech or behavior that purposefully deceives or misleads others through lies or trickery

deceive – to cause to believe something is not true or valid

decision – act of resolving a question or issue or of choosing between two or more courses of action

effect – something brought about by something else

exchange – the action or instance of giving or receiving one thing for another

exist – to have actual being at a particular point in time

expect – to anticipate or think likely

favor – to treat with preference or partiality

general – concerned with, applicable to, or affecting the whole

government – the set of formal legal institutions that are formed to administer and manage the affairs of a nation or other political community

honorable – having or showing strict adherence to what is morally right and lawful

illegal – forbidden by law or edict

immoral – not in accord with moral standards

impact – to have direct effect

improper – not appropriate, suitable, or correct

influence – a power to change a someone's belief or behavior or to affect a course of events without exerting direct control or apparent effort

influence peddling – use of real or potential influence on someone's behalf in exchange for money or favors

information – facts or ideas received or given

insider trading – the act of basing personal investment decisions on confidential or privileged information

institution – a significant and established organization

investment – an asset acquired for the purpose of producing future wealth

lawful – allowed or not prohibited by law

lie – a statement made with deliberate intent to deceive

loyal – faithful to a person or cause, steadfast in allegiance

mislead – to give a wrong impression or guide toward a wrong conclusion

money – medium of exchange with unit value equal to the goods and services that can be acquired for it

moral – adhering to standards of responsible, respectful, and fair behavior

negative – undesirable, unfavorable, or detrimental

opinion – belief about something that may or may not be based on fact or knowledge

partial – bias toward or preference for one thing over another

partisan – a ardent supporter or advocate of a party, faction, or cause

person – an individual human being

personal – anything that relates or pertains to an individual person's own self

political – relating to public affairs and governance

political patronage – appointment or hiring of someone on the basis of partisan loyalty to fill a government position

position – one's role and importance in an organization or in society

potential – capable of being but not yet in existence

power – being able to do what one wants; having the ability to control people or things

practice – something done regularly or constantly

privileged – available or limited to only one or a few

purpose – the objective toward which one strives

purposefully – mindful of the objective toward which one strives

realistic – having an awareness of things as they actually are rather than as they are imagined or desired to be

right – conforms with ethical and moral principles

significant – important and deserving of attention

social – relating to the way people live together and interact with others

social institution – an entity formed to meet a societal need or preserve a societal value

society – a system of human organization that supplies protection, continuity, security, and identity

strict – stringent in requirement or control

success – favorable or desirable outcome

think – to use one's mind to remember, ponder, imagine, plan, decide, or otherwise produce thought

trickery – pretense or crafty ingenuity to deceive or cheat

unlawful – not allowed by law

wrong – not in accord with ethical and moral principles

DECEIT

speech or behavior that purposefully deceives or misleads others through lies or trickery

---

DISTRACTION
something that diverts attention from something else

EDITORIALIZING
presenting, expressing, or promoting a point of view

HYPERBOLE
an exaggerated statement made to emphasize something stated, evoke strong feelings, or create a forceful impression

FALSEHOOD
an untrue statement, not consistent with truth or fact

HIDDEN AGENDA

secret or unadmitted reason for doing something while claiming or appearing to do something else

BAIT AND SWITCH

the unethical practice of offering for sale something that is never intended to be sold or produced in order to create an opportunity to sell something that is substantially different and less desirable

PROPAGANDA

information, especially of a prejudiced, misleading, or untrue nature, used to promote or publicize a particular cause or point of view

STIPULATIVE DEFINITION

purports to describe the commonly accepted meaning of a term, but actually specifies an uncommon or altered use

STRAWMAN DEFINITION

a misrepresented or distorted position or opinion that is easier to attack or refute than the original and actual position or opinion

PROJECTION

falsely and maliciously claiming that one's own beliefs or point of view are those of another person or group of people

CENSORSHIP

the act, process, or practice of prohibiting or suppressing communication of information that presents an unwelcome point of view

SCAREMONGERING

the action of creating or spreading stories that make people feel worried or fearful

GASLIGHTING

the action of causing others to question or doubt their memories, beliefs, or judgment

BRAINWASHING

intensive indoctrination aimed at reducing a person's ability to think critically or independently and replacing their basic attitudes, values, and beliefs with an alternative set of attitudes, values, and beliefs

---

1. Do you think that a strong desire for power and control is naturally linked to an inclination and willingness to deceive? Why or why not?

2. Do you or do you not think it is generally realistic to expect people who engage in one form of deceit or another form of corruption to be deceitful and corrupt in other ways as well? Why?

3. To what extent do you agree with the notion that actions speak louder than words?

4. Do you or do you not think you are sufficiently aware of what is happening in the world around you? Why?

5. Do you think that you are sufficiently skeptical about what you hear and read? Why or why not?

6. How do you determine whether what you hear and read is actually true and fairly stated?

7. Are there public figures who you believe are deceitful or otherwise corrupt? On what do you base your opinion?

8. To what extent do you think deceitful behavior can be tolerated within a generally moral society? To what extent are you personally willing to tolerate deceitful behavior?

---

ability – the capacity, knowledge, and skill to do something

act – to do something

action – something done or accomplished

actual – existing in fact or reality

admit – to disclose or agree that something is true

alter – to make something different in some way

alternative – one of two or more choices or courses of action

attention – notice, awareness, or consideration

attitude – the general way of thinking, feeling, or behaving that reflects a person's state of mind or disposition

aware – having or showing realization or perception

bait and switch – the unethical practice of offering for sale something that is never intended to be sold or produced in order to create an opportunity to sell something that is substantially different and less desirable

behavior – the way one acts or conducts oneself

belief – a person's conviction about the truth, existence, or validity of something

brainwashing – intensive indoctrination aimed at reducing a person's ability to think critically or independently and replacing their basic attitudes, values, and beliefs with an alternative set of attitudes, values, and beliefs

cause – a principle or purpose that inspires human action

censorship – the act, process, or practice of prohibiting or suppressing communication of information that presents an unwelcome point of view

claim – assertion or asserting that is something is true or fact

common – familiar or typical

consistent – free from variation

control – to exercise authoritative power or dominating influence

corrupt – unlawful, improper, or immoral in character or conduct

create – to cause to exist or bring into being

critical – using skilled and careful judgment

deceit – speech or behavior that purposefully deceives or misleads others through lies or trickery

deceive – to cause to believe something is not true or valid

deception – act of causing someone to believe something that is misleading or hides the truth

desire – something wanted or wished for

determine – to identify, establish, or decide

distort – to twist or change from original shape or meaning

distraction – something that diverts attention from something else

divert – to cause someone or something to turn from one thing to another

editorializing – presenting, expressing, or promoting a point of view

emphasize – to show something is important or deserves special attention

engage – to come together or to take part in something

entice – to attract, usually by arousing hope, interest, or desire

evoke – to provoke strong feelings

exaggerate – to characterize something as larger, more important, better, or worse than it actually is

expect – to anticipate or think likely

expertise – high degree of skill in or knowledge about a particular subject

extent – the range, distance, space, or magnitude of something

fact – something that is consistent with objective reality and can be proven to be true

fair – absence of bias, impartial

false – contrary to fact or truth

falsehood – an untrue statement, not consistent with truth or fact

fear – an often strong emotion caused by threat or awareness of real or imagined danger

feeling – an emotional state or reaction

force – the capacity to cause change

form – the shape or structure of something

gaslighting – the action of causing others to question or doubt their memories, beliefs, or judgment

general – concerned with, applicable to, or affecting the whole

group – a number of similar individuals or things considered together as one

hidden agenda – secret or unadmitted reason for doing something while claiming or appearing to do something else

hyperbole – an exaggerated statement made to emphasize something stated, evoke strong feelings, or create a forceful impression

impression – an indistinct but consequential notion or remembrance

inclination – a preference for thinking or acting in a particular way

independent – free from dominance or control of others, relying on one's own judgment, capabilities, or resources

indoctrination – continuously repeating and promoting a doctrine, principle, or ideology until it is accepted without doubt as being true

information – facts or ideas received or given

intense – existing in a high or extreme degree

judgment – the ability to make considered decisions or come to sensible conclusions

knowledge – information acquired through experience, schooling, or study

lie – a statement made with deliberate intent to deceive

link – to connect one thing with another

malicious – intentionally and purposefully causing harm

misrepresent – to describe or depict something falsely or incorrectly

moral – adhering to standards of responsible, respectful, and fair behavior

natural – existing in or formed by nature

nature – the inherent character or basic constitution of a person or thing

notion – vague or imprecise impression or idea

opinion – belief about something that may or may not be based on fact or knowledge

original – the first instance of something

particular – reference to a single person or thing rather than to others

person – an individual human being

personal – anything that relates or pertains to an individual person's own self

point of view – the perspective from which we view and explain something

position – a person's firm belief or point of view

power – having the ability to control people or things

practice – something done regularly or constantly

prejudice – having or showing an unfair or unreasonable opinion or feeling, especially when formed without logical thought and relevant knowledge

process – a series of tasks done to accomplish a particular result

prohibit – to officially forbid or refuse to allow something

projection – falsely and maliciously claiming that one's own beliefs or point of view are those of another person or group of people

promote – to help or encourage to exist or flourish

propaganda – information, especially of a prejudiced, misleading, or untrue nature, used to promote or publicize a particular cause or point of view

publicize – to cause public awareness

purport – to have or present an often false appearance or intention

purposefully – mindful of the objective toward which one strives

realistic – having an awareness of things as they actually are rather than as they are imagined or desired to be

reason – the basis or motive for an action, decision, or belief

reduce – to make or become smaller

refute – to show or prove that something is false or erroneous

scaremongering – the action of creating or spreading stories that make people feel worried or fearful

set – a group of similar or related things

skeptical – a doubting or questioning attitude or state of mind

society – a system of human organization that supplies protection, continuity, security, and identity

specify – to identify or to state clearly

statement – a description, assertion, or declaration

stipulate – to specify, demand, or concede something in particular

stipulative definition – purports to describe the commonly accepted meaning of a term, but actually specifies an uncommon or altered use

strawman definition – a misrepresented or distorted position or opinion that is easier to attack or refute than the original and actual position or opinion

sufficient – having as much as is needed

support – to serve as a foundation

suppress – to curtail or prevent something from being seen or expressed

term – a word or expression that when used contextually has precise meaning

think – to use one's mind to remember, ponder, imagine, plan, decide, or otherwise produce thought

tolerate – to permit something to exist without prohibition or interference

trickery – pretense or crafty ingenuity to deceive or cheat

true – that which exists in accordance with fact or reality

untrue – not true, contrary to fact, false

values – personal beliefs that guide individual behavior

world – the earthly state of human existence

PROGRESS

movement toward improved quality of life and standard of living

PROSPERITY

the condition of being wealthy or successful

QUALITY OF LIFE
a subjective assessment of overall enjoyment of life

STANDARD OF LIVING
the level of material comfort experienced by a person or community

MARKET ECONOMY

an economic system that relies mostly on market forces to determine prices and allocate resources and goods and services

PLANNED ECONOMY

an economic system that relies mostly on government agencies to allocate goods and resources and determine prices

INCREMENTAL INCENTIVE

an incitement to act that is characterized by the incremental benefits of taking action exceeding its incremental costs

COMMON GOOD

the condition of all people in a society or group having legitimate, fair, and equal opportunities to achieve personal success

MORALITY

relating to or concerned with the standards of personal behavior

ENVY

resentful awareness of the good luck, qualities, or possessions of another person

1. In what ways do you believe incremental incentives affect the operations and success of market economies and planned economies? Do credible historical accounts support your opinion?

2. Do you think in a free market economic system that the prices of goods and services are generally based on what it costs to produce them or on what people are willing to pay for them? On what facts do you base your opinion?

3. Do you think that people in the bottom five percent of society today enjoy a higher standard of living than did those in the top five percent of society one hundred years ago? Why or why not? Is your perception fact-based?

4. Do you think there is a more correct definition of the term "common good" than "the condition of all people in a society or group having legitimate, fair, and equal opportunities to achieve personal success?" If so, how do the two definitions differ?

5. Do you think that a society whose members are generally moral people is or is not more likely to prosper than a society whose members are generally immoral people? Why?

6. Do you think the statement "envy is the most corrosive of all human emotions" is correct? Why or why not?

---

achieve – to accomplish something important

act – to do something

action – something done or accomplished

affect – to act on or cause change

agency – a government or administrative organization

allocate – to assign or set apart

assessment – the action or product of determining the value, significance, or extent of something

aware – having or showing realization or perception

believe – to accept the truth, existence, or validity of something

benefit – something that produces helpful results or that promotes or enhances well-being

characterize – to describe the qualities or peculiarities of a person or thing

comfort – the condition or cause of feeling pleasurable ease or relief

common good – the condition of all people in a society or group having legitimate, fair, and equal opportunities to achieve personal success

community – a group of people who live in a particular geographical area or who share common interests or points of view

concern – the act of being attentive to or caring about something

condition – a state of existence as determined by a set of circumstances

correct – in agreement with truth or facts, or in compliance with what is generally accepted

corrosive – gradually destructive and steadily harmful

cost – money or other resource expended to acquire, produce, or maintain something

credible – capable of being trusted

definition – a brief explanation of the meaning of a word or phrase

determine – to identify, establish, or decide

economic – relating to production, distribution, and consumption of goods and services

emotion – a spontaneous mental reaction experienced as a strong feeling

envy – resentful awareness of the good luck, qualities, or possessions of another person

equal – of the same importance, quality, or amount

experience – doing, seeing, or feeling something

fact – something that is consistent with objective reality and can be proven to be true

fair – absence of bias, impartial

force – the capacity to cause change

general – concerned with, applicable to, or affecting the whole

good – satisfactory as to quality, quantity, or degree

goods and services – reference to tangible items such as commodities, equipment, materials, or supplies (goods) and work that is done on behalf of or for the benefit of others (services)

government – the set of formal legal institutions that are formed to administer and manage the affairs of a nation or other political community

group – a number of similar individuals or things considered together as one

history – the study of past events and how they relate to human behavior

immoral – not in accord with moral standards

incite – to move or provoke to action

incremental – denoting a usually small positive or negative change in a variable quantity

incremental incentive – an incitement to act that is characterized by the incremental benefits of taking action exceeding its incremental costs

legitimate – reasonable and acceptable

life – all of the experiences and actions that constitute a person's existence

luck – the chance happening of good fortune or adversity

market – a gathering where buyers and sellers exchange goods and services

market economy – an economic system that relies mostly on market forces to determine prices and allocate resources and goods and services

material – having importance or consequence

moral – adhering to standards of responsible, respectful, and fair behavior

morality – relating to or concerned with the standards of personal behavior

movement – motion or development

operation – some form of work or production

opinion – belief about something that may or may not be based on fact or knowledge

opportunity – a situation which makes it possible to do something in particular

overall – in general rather than in particular

perception – comprehension or understanding of something

personal – anything that relates or pertains to an individual person's own self

planned economy – an economic system that relies mostly on government agencies to allocate goods and resources and determine prices

possess – to have under one's power or control

price – the amount paid for goods or services

progress – movement toward improved quality of life and standard of living

prosper – to have success or financial well-being

prosperity – the condition of being wealthy or successful

quality – level of excellence

quality of life – a subjective assessment of overall enjoyment of life

relate – to have connection or reference

rely – to depend on or place trust in

resent – to feel displeased or aggrieved due to a sense of being treated unjustly

resource – something that has utility or that is available for use

respectful – feeling or showing due regard and tolerance for self and others

responsible – accountable for own conduct; dependable and trustworthy

society – a system of human organization that supplies protection, continuity, security, and identity

standard – an established or acceptable measure of value, quality, or quantity

standard of living – the level of material comfort experienced by a person or group of people

statement – a description, assertion, or declaration

subjective – influenced by or based on beliefs and feelings

success – favorable or desirable outcome; accomplishment of something desired, planned, or attempted

successful – the condition of having done something desired, planned, or attempted

support – to serve as a foundation; to provide substantiation

system – interacting, interrelated, or interdependent elements that form or function as a whole

term – a word or expression that when used contextually has precise meaning

think – to use one's mind to remember, ponder, imagine, plan, decide, or otherwise produce thought

wealthy – the state or condition of having significant resources

MERITOCRACY

a social system, society, or organization in which individual personal success is dependent on demonstrated value, ability, or achievement rather than on social class, credentials, tenure, intent, personal character or connections, privilege, or celebrity

---

MERIT
demonstrated value, ability, or achievement

CREDENTIALS
degrees, certifications, and licenses issued by schools, professional organizations, and government entities

---

1. Do you think people sometimes use the word "merit" when they mean "credentials"? If so, why do you think this occurs?

2. Would you favor or oppose our society being structured and operating as a genuine meritocracy? Why?

3. If our society were structured and operated as a genuine meritocracy, do you think it would cause most people to change their behavior? Why or why not? Would it cause you to change your behavior? If so, in what ways?

4. Do you think the core principle of meritocracy coincides or is in conflict with the laws of nature? In what ways?

5. Do you think that a society structured and operated as a meritocracy would likely be a generally moral society? Why or why not?

6. Do you think that a society structured and operated as a meritocracy would likely be a prosperous society? Why or why not?

---

ability – the capacity, knowledge, and skill to do something

achieve – to accomplish something important

behavior – the way one acts or conducts oneself

cause – something that brings about something else

celebrity – a famous or well-known person

change – the act or instance of becoming different

coincide – to match or correspond exactly in nature, character, or function

concern – the act of being attentive to or caring about something

conflict – a state of disagreement or disharmony

continuity – uninterrupted extension in space, time, or sequence

core – the most essential or enduring part of something

credentials – degrees, certifications, and licenses issued by schools, professional organizations, and government entities

demonstrate – to make evident or show clearly

dependent – determined or decided by someone or something else

fair – absence of bias, impartial

favor – to treat with preference or partiality

general – concerned with, applicable to, or affecting the whole

genuine – actually possessing reputed qualities or character, authentic

group – a number of similar individuals or things considered together as one

human – reference to the species *homo sapiens*

identity – the distinguishing beliefs, characteristics, or qualities of a person or group of people

individual – reference to a single human being or other single distinct entity

intent – desire or will to do something

interdependent – influenced or impacted by each other

laws of nature – the uniformity of natural instincts, actions, and relationships of organic beings

likely – probably will happen or is expected to happen

merit – demonstrated value, ability, or achievement

meritocracy – a social system, society, or organization in which individual personal success is dependent on demonstrated value, ability, or achievement rather than on social class, credentials, tenure, intent, personal character or connections, privilege, or celebrity

moral – adhering to standards of responsible, respectful, and fair behavior

morality – relating to or concerned with the standards of personal behavior

operate – to perform or function

oppose – to be in conflict with or act against

organization – a group of people who work together in a structured way for a particular purpose; spontaneous or deliberate formation of arrangement or order

personal – anything that relates or pertains to an individual person's own self

principle – a fundamental truth that serves as a foundational tenet of a system of beliefs or a chain of reasoning

privilege – special entitlement granted to an individual or group that benefits only the individual or group and not society as a whole

prosper – to have success or financial well-being

protect – to defend or shield against injury, harm, or loss

relate – to have connection or reference

respectful – feeling or showing due regard and tolerance for self and others

responsible – accountable for own conduct; dependable and trustworthy

security – free from actual risk or danger

social – relating to the way people live together and interact with others

social class – a group of people of similar status, rank, or common characteristics within a society who possess the same socioeconomic status

society – a system of human organization that supplies protection, continuity, security, and identity

structure – the way parts are put together to form a whole

success – favorable or desirable outcome

supply – to provide or make available

system – interacting, interrelated, or interdependent elements that form or function as a whole

tenure – the length of time that a person remains in a position or job

think – to use one's mind to remember, ponder, imagine, plan, decide, or otherwise produce thought

use – to put into action or service or employ for a purpose

value – the usefulness or importance of someone or something

worth – the character or intrinsic qualities of someone or something

GLOSSARY

a dictionary of limited scope

VOCABULARY
fundamental tool for communication and acquiring knowledge

WORD
a unit of language that conveys meaning

CONTEXT
the discourse that surrounds a word and determines its meaning

---

ability – the capacity, knowledge, and skill to do something

absence – the condition of not being present

absolute – complete or without restriction

abstract – existing as an idea, feeling, or quality considered generally rather than specifically

abstract thinking – ability to think in terms of principles and generalizations

academia – the community and culture of those engaged in higher education teaching and research

acceptable – suitable to meet a need or standard

accomplish – to do something successfully

accord – to be in agreement, conformity, or harmony

accountable – subject to an obligation to report, explain, or justify one's behavior

accurate – without error or defect

achieve – to accomplish something important

acquire – to gain or come into ownership or possession of something

act – to do something

action – something done or accomplished

activity – something requiring physical or mental effort that one or many engage in doing

actual – existing in fact or reality

adapt – to make fit for a particular situation or use

adhere – to be attached or to remain devoted

administer – to direct or oversee the operation of something

admire – to regard with approval, esteem, or pleasure

admit – to disclose or agree that something is true

adopt – to voluntarily choose to accept, follow, or take into a relationship

advanced – being at a higher level or more highly developed

advantage – anything that makes doing something easier to do or more likely to happen

adversity – bad luck or unfavorable fortune or fate

advertising – promoting or creating awareness about a product, service, or cause

affair – something done or experienced; a matter of commercial, professional, public, or personal interest or concern

affect – to act on or cause change

agency – a government or administrative organization

agreement – being alike in opinion or action

alignment – a favorably arranged state of mutual support

allocate – to assign or set apart

allow – to permit or let happen

alter – to make something different in some way

alternative – one of two or more choices or courses of action

altruistic – concerned for the welfare of others

amenable – willing to submit to authority

amusement – anything that pleases or entertains

analysis – careful and methodical thought

analytic thinking – way of thinking that is based on systematic analysis of data or situation

analyze – to examine something in a careful and methodical way

ancestor – a person from whom one is descended

apply – to put something to use or to put one thing on top of another

appoint – to assign to an office or position

aptitude – a natural capacity for learning

arbitrary – unrestrained and autocratic in the use of authority or power

area – a geographic region, a part of the earth's surface

arrogant – having or showing an exaggerated or pretentious sense of one's own importance, abilities, or understanding

aspect – a particular characteristic or feature of a person or thing

assessment – the action or product of determining the value, significance, or extent of something

assimilation – the act or process of absorbing and incorporating into the whole

association – an organization of people; being involved with or connected to someone or something

assure – to make certain or cause to feel certain

athletic aptitude – capacity to perform physical activities that require agility, dexterity, strength, swiftness, or other similar qualities

attention – notice, awareness, or consideration

attitude – the general way of thinking, feeling, or behaving that reflects a person's state of mind or disposition

attribute – to regard as a quality, characteristic, or measure of a person or thing

authoritarian – favoring or enforcing strict obedience to those in positions of power

authoritarianism – a system in which a single person or a small group of people possess mostly unlimited control or influence

authority – power or right to direct, control, or command; a person or group of people that has the power or right to direct, control, or command

autocrat – a ruler with unlimited power or authority

available – accessible and ready for use

average – a standard or level that is considered to be representative or typical of the whole of something

avoid – to purposefully stay away from something

award – to grant or bestow as being merited, deserved, or needed

aware – having or showing realization or perception

bait and switch – the unethical practice of offering for sale something that is never intended to be sold or produced in order to create an opportunity to sell something that is substantially different and less desirable

balance – a condition of equilibrium produced by proper distribution of counteracting forces

basic – constituting, forming, or serving as a base element or starting point

basis – something that underlies, supports, or is essential to something else

behavior – the way one acts or conducts oneself

being – the fact of existence; a living thing

belief – a person's conviction about the truth, existence, or validity of something

believe – to accept the truth, existence, or validity of something

benefactor – one who confers a benefit on another

benefit – something that produces helpful results or that promotes or enhances well-being

bias – inclination or tendency to favor one over another

biased – having or showing an unjust or unfair opinion or feeling about someone or something

biological – pertaining to genetic lineage

biology – the study of organisms and their life processes

book – a bound text in printed form

bound – the condition of being obligated, limited, or restrained

bribe – money or favor given or received to secure preferential treatment

bribery – the act of giving or taking a bribe

brutal – ruthless or unrelenting

business – the activity of buying and selling commodities, products, or services; an organization engaged in commercial, industrial, or professional activities; an occupation, profession, or trade

capable – having the capacity and ability needed to do something

capacity – the potential to learn or retain knowledge; availability, power, or fitness to act

careful – cautious in one's actions, attentive to potential danger, error, or harm

causation – the relationship between cause and effect; act or process of making something happen

cause – something that brings about something else; a principle or purpose that inspires human action

cause and effect – the relationship between two things in which one is the result of the other

celebrity – a famous or well-known person

censorship – the act, process, or practice of prohibiting or suppressing communication of information that presents an unwelcome point of view

central – principal or dominant thing on which related things depend

certainty – the quality of being known or proven to be true

chain reaction – a series of events in which each event causes or influences the next subsequent event

chance – the unknown and unpredictable aspect of happenings that cannot be foreseen or controlled

change – the act or instance of becoming different; to alter or modify

character – moral or ethical quality; the characteristics of people that make them distinct from other people

characteristic – a distinguishing or distinctive feature

characterize – to describe the qualities or peculiarities of a person or thing

choice – something that is selected from a set of possibilities

choices – the options from which something is selected

choose – to select after consideration

circumstance – a determining factor or set of factors

citizen – a person who due to birth or naturalization has a specific legal relationship with a state or nation

civil liberties – individual rights that governments commit not to abridge either by legislation or judicial interpretation

civility – the quality or act of being courteous or polite

civilization – advanced stage of human social and economic development and organization

civilized – marked by well-organized laws and rules about how people interact with one another; being polite, reasonable, and respectful

claim – to take or ask for, especially as a right; assertion or asserting that something is true or fact

clarity – clearness or lucidity as to perception or understanding

code – a system of principles or rules

codify – to establish or recognize individual rights, statutes, rules, or regulations

cognition – mental activity of acquiring, recalling, or using knowledge

cognitive – relating to mental activities of thinking, reasoning, or remembering

coincide – to match or correspond exactly in nature, character, or function

collaboratively – an effort or way in which people work together

collective – some number of people acting as a group; done by people acting as a group

collectivism – belief that the priorities of a group, somehow decided, should be favored over the dignity and welfare of the individual

collusion – cooperation for an illegal or deceitful purpose

combine – the act of joining or mixing two or more things to form a separate thing

comfort – the condition or cause of feeling pleasurable ease or relief

common – belonging to or shared by members of a community; familiar or typical

common good – the condition of all people in a society or group having legitimate, fair, and equal opportunities to achieve personal success

common sense – sound and prudent judgment based on insight and intuition

communicate – to share information or knowledge

community – a group of people who live in a particular geographical area or who share common interests or points of view

company – a business that produces or sells goods or services

comparable – being enough alike to be considered generally equivalent

competent – having skills or knowledge needed for effective conduct or action

competition – a rivalry for supremacy or advantage

complementary – the characteristic of what enables a person or thing to enhance the strengths and compensate for the weaknesses of another

complex – something that is made up of interdependent parts or elements whose dependencies may be imperfectly known or are unknowable

complicated – something that is difficult to understand, often involving intricately combined parts

comprehend – to grasp or perceive the nature or meaning of something

comprehensive – inclusive of all or much

comprise – to include, contain, or consist of

conceit – an arrogant assumption of superiority; an excessively favorable opinion of one's own abilities, value, or worth

concentrated – collected together in a single place

concept – a generalized or abstract notion or understanding of something

conception – the process of forming an idea or abstraction

concern – the act of being attentive to or caring about something

concrete – reference to the reality of an actual thing or instance

concrete thinking – cognition centered on objects or ideas as specific items rather than as principles and generalizations

condition – a state of existence as determined by a set of circumstances

conduct – personal behavior, way of acting, or bearing or deportment

confident – certain or self-assured

confidential – strictly private or secret

conflict – a state of disagreement or disharmony

conform – to comply with a set of standards, expectations, or specifications

confusion – the condition of being unable to distinguish one from another

conscious – focused on or being aware of something in particular

conscious mind – refers to the capacity of the human mind to acquire knowledge and understanding and act in a thoughtful way

consequence – an effect, result, or outcome; the importance or relevance of something

consider – to regard or believe, or to think carefully about something

consideration – careful, deliberate thought

consistent – free from variation

constant – continuously occurring or recurring

constitute – to make up or form the completeness of something

constitution – the structure, composition, physical makeup, or nature of something; a written instrument embodying the rules of a political or social organization

constraint – a limiting or controlling condition

contentment – being at ease in one's situation, without desire for change

context – the discourse that surrounds a word and determines its meaning

continuity – uninterrupted extension in space, time, or sequence

continuous – uninterrupted or unending

contrary – a fact or condition mutually opposed to another fact or condition

control – to exercise authoritative power or dominating influence

conviction – a fixed or firm belief

cooperation – willingly working with others or acting together for a common purpose or benefit

core – the most essential or enduring part of something

correct – in agreement with truth or facts, or in compliance with what is generally accepted

corrosive – gradually destructive and steadily harmful

corrupt – unlawful, improper, or immoral in character or conduct

cost – money or other resource expended to acquire, produce, or maintain something

counteract – to reduce or remove the effect of something by bringing to bear a contrary influence

create – to cause to exist or bring into being

credentials – degrees, certifications, and licenses issued by schools, professional organizations, and government entities

credible – capable of being trusted

criteria – the rules or ideals by which something is judged or assessed

critical – using skilled and careful judgment; indispensable or vital

critical thinking skills – ability to gather, interpret, and objectively evaluate and analyze information as the means to solve problems, make decisions, and form judgments

criticize – to find fault or express disapproval of someone or something

cronyism – the practice of showing partiality to friends or allies

crucial – vital or very significant and important

cults – social groups defined by their religious, spiritual, political, or philosophical beliefs, or by common interest in a particular personality, object, or unachievable goal

culture – shared pattern of behavior and understanding that is learned through socialization

cumulative – sum of incremental amounts

current – occurring in or existing at the present time

custom – a long-standing and common way of doing something

dangerous – involving possible injury, harm, or loss

deceit – speech or behavior that purposefully deceives or misleads others through lies or trickery

deceive – to cause to believe something is not true or valid

deception – act of causing someone to believe something that is misleading or hides the truth

decision – act of resolving a question or issue or of choosing between two or more courses of action

definition – a brief explanation of the meaning of a word or phrase

degree – any of the series of steps or stages in a progression, process, or course of action

deliberate – characterized by careful and thorough thought and consideration

delusion – belief in something that is false

demonstrate – to make evident or show clearly

dependable – consistently behaves or acts in an expected and sensible way

dependent – determined or decided by someone or something else; the quality of relying on the judgment, capabilities, or resources of others

derive – to take, receive, or obtain from a specific source

descend – to originate or come from an ancestral source

deserve – to be worthy

designed social processes – social processes that are formed and arbitrarily imposed on society by a ruling class

desirable – worth wanting, doing, or achieving

desire – something wanted or wished for

destructive – causing ruin or devastation

determination – firm or fixed intention to accomplish a desired result

determine – to identify, establish, or decide

develop – to grow into or bring to a more mature, advanced, or effective state

devotion – profound dedication, loyalty, or affection

dictionary – a collection of words or terms and their meanings

different – not alike in nature, form, or quality

difficult – hard to do or hard to deal with

diffuse – to weaken or make less intense

dignity – the worth and value of a person

dimension – one of a set of elements or factors that constitute a complete existence, personality, or consciousness

direct causation – a cause and effect relationship in which no events or things intervene between the cause and effect

discourse – verbal exchange or conversation in speech or writing

discrete – constituting a separate and distinct thing

dishonest – disposed to lie, cheat, defraud, or deceive

disorder – a state or condition of turmoil or confusion

disposition – usual mood or attitude, inclination to think act in a particular way

disrespectful – feeling or showing a lack of tolerance or civility

disruptive – causing disorder, turmoil, or an interruption in the way something usually is done or happens

distinct – clearly separate and different

distinguish – to understand, recognize, or notice differences between people or things

distort – to twist or change from original shape or meaning

distraction – something that diverts attention from something else

distribute – to place or put into position; to allocate to several or many

diversity – the quality or condition of being different

divert – to cause someone or something to turn from one thing to another

dominance – primacy, rule, or control

dominant – commanding, controlling, or prevailing over all others

dominate – to control or rule

duality – the condition of having or combining two different or opposite things

due – fair and proper

earned – acquired in exchange for work done

economic – relating to production, distribution, and consumption of goods and services

economics – the study of how allocations and uses of scarce resources affect human behavior and well-being

editorializing – presenting, expressing, or promoting a point of view

education – the action or process of teaching and learning; the knowledge, skills, values, beliefs, and habits learned from observation, study, and experience

effect – something brought about by something else

effective – the degree of success in producing a desired result; skilled or able to do something well

efficient – the degree of success in doing something with least waste of time and energy

effort – a conscious exertion of energy to do something

elation – a feeling or state of bliss or great joy

element – a constituent part

eliminate – to remove or omit

embrace – to accept something enthusiastically

emotion – a spontaneous mental reaction experienced as a strong feeling

emphasize – to show something is important or deserves special attention

enable – to provide with means or opportunity, to make possible

encourage – to influence or help motivate someone to do something

energy – power expended to cause or enable change

engage – to come together or to take part in something

enhance – to improve the quality or value of something

enliven – to make more interesting or exciting

entice – to attract, usually by arousing hope, interest, or desire

entitled – being or believing oneself to be deserving of special treatment

entitlement – certain benefits or privileges to which one has a right or claim

entity – something that exists as a discrete unit

envision – to conceive or see in one's mind

envy – resentful awareness of the good luck, qualities, or possessions of another person

equal – of the same importance, quality, or amount

equality – the condition or quality of all members of a society being equal, specifically as it relates to the rights and opportunities of each individual

equilibrium – the condition of all things influencing the stability of a person or thing being offset or cancelled out by the forces of other influences

equity – the state or condition of all members of a society being treated in an equal and just way; redefined by progressives as somehow assuring exactly equal outcome for each person, regardless of personal intellect, interests, abilities, or behavior

error – an assertion or belief that unintentionally deviates from what is right or true

essential – absolutely necessary, indispensable

establish – to bring about or set into place

established – long recognized and widely accepted

esteem – to admire or regard favorably

ethics – one's own moral philosophy or a personal code of conduct; branch of philosophy dealing with values relating to human conduct

evaluate – to analyze or establish the quality, importance, or value of something

event – something that takes place, especially a significant occurrence

evil – morally bad or sinful

evoke – to provoke strong feelings

evolve – to change or develop gradually

evolved social processes – systemically formed social processes that adapt spontaneously to the needs of society

excellent – highest or finest quality, exceptionally good

exceptional – far above average, uncommon, extraordinary

excessive – more than what is usual, proper, or necessary

exchange – the action or instance of giving or receiving one thing for another

exclusive – available or limited to only one or a few

excuse – attempt to explain or justify what turns out to have been an ill-considered action, decision, or belief

exercise – to act or bring into play; something done to develop or maintain ability or understanding

exist – to have actual being at a particular point in time

existence – the state or fact of having actual being at a particular point in time

expect – to anticipate or think likely

experience – doing, seeing, or feeling something

expertise – high degree of skill in or knowledge about a particular subject

exploit – to selfishly take advantage of

extent – the range, distance, space, or magnitude of something

external – something that exists or happens outside or apart from itself

extreme – far exceeding the ordinary or usual

extrinsic – something originating or derived from outside itself

extrovert – a person who is naturally inclined to maximize social engagement

fact – something that is consistent with objective reality and can be proven to be true

factor – something that has an effect on a circumstance or situation

faculty – the capacity or ability to act or do something

failure – unfavorable or undesirable outcome

fair – absence of bias, impartial

faith – unwavering or unshakeable belief without proof or evidence

false – contrary to fact or truth

falsehood – an untrue statement, not consistent with truth or fact

familiar – acquainted, often encountered or seen

family – a group of people who are biologically or legally related to one another

fanatical – having or showing extreme devotion to some usually social or religious ideal or goal

fantasy – something that is created by and exists only in the imagination

fate – a power, force, or principle that is believed to cause things to happen as they do

faulty thinking – a biased or illogical way of using one's mind

favor – to treat with preference or partiality

favorable – helpful, tending to promote or facilitate

fear – an often strong emotion caused by threat or awareness of real or imagined danger

feature – an important part of something

feeling – an emotional state or reaction; a mostly vague and imprecisely sourced belief

feudalism – a political, social, and economic system in which people in the lower social classes are awarded limited property rights by people of higher rank and in return work and fight for their supposed benefactors

firm – not soft or yielding, but not hard; securely or solidly fixed in place

firmness – being securely or solidly fixed in place

flourish – to do well or be in a vigorous state

focus – to concentrate on or pay particular attention to something

foolish – silly or unwise, having or showing a lack of common sense, good judgment, or discretion

force – the capacity to cause change

forgive – to pardon an offense or offender or to eliminate consequence

form – to bring into existence or to shape or mold; the shape or structure of something

formal – official or proper form or structure

fortune – the chance and unpredictable happening of favorable and unfavorable events

foster – to nurture, promote growth or development

found – to bring into existence, set up, or establish

foundation – the base on which something stands

fracture – to divide or to damage or destroy

free – without restraint or restriction; having personal rights or individual liberty; made available at no charge

freedom – the unhindered right to think, speak, and act however one wants

fulfill – to carry out or bring to realization

function – the specific action or purpose for which a person or thing is designed, used, or exists

fundamental – forming or serving as an essential component of a concept, system, or structure

funds – a sum of money or other similar resource

gaslighting – the action of causing others to question or doubt their memories, beliefs, or judgment

general – concerned with, applicable to, or affecting the whole

generalization – a statement that summarizes an idea or impression

genetics – the physical and causal factors of heredity

genuine – actually possessing reputed qualities or character, authentic

geographical – relating to a particular place or area on the earth's surface

given – the act or instance of transferring ownership or possession of something to another

glossary – a dictionary of limited scope

goal – the object of ambition or effort or a desired result

good – satisfactory as to quality, quantity, or degree; morally excellent

goods and services – reference to tangible items such as commodities, equipment, materials, or supplies (goods) and work that is done on behalf of or for the benefit of others (services)

governance – the act or process of governing or overseeing the control and direction of a society or an organization

government – the set of formal legal institutions that are formed to administer and manage the affairs of a nation or other political community

grant – to bestow, confer, or allow

group – a number of similar individuals or things considered together as one

groupthink – the phenomenon of being influenced by peers to adopt uninformed or illogical opinions and behaviors that are common within a community to which one is connected

guarantee – a promise or assurance of specific performance, quality, or benefit

gullible – easily deceived, fooled, or cheated

happiness – a positive state of mind, attitude, or feeling about how one is living and has lived one's life

happy – feeling satisfaction, contentment, and joy

harm – to do or cause physical or psychological damage or injury; an immoral or unjust effect

harmony – absence of conflict

hidden agenda – secret or unadmitted reason for doing something while claiming or appearing to do something else

history – the study of past events and how they relate to human behavior

hobby – an activity in which one engages mainly for pleasure or relaxation

honest – free of deceit and untruthfulness to self and others

honorable – having or showing strict adherence to what is morally right and lawful

hope – to want something that one considers possible to happen or be true

hubris – extreme or foolish pride, conceit, or dangerous overconfidence

human – a person; reference to the species *homo sapiens*

humanity – the whole existence of the human species

humble – modest in behavior and attitude; aware of inherent limitations and imperfections of human beings

hyperbole – an exaggerated statement made to emphasize something stated, evoke strong feelings, or create a forceful impression

idea – a thought or opinion that is the product of mental understanding, awareness, or activity

ideal – a conception of something that in its absolute perfection exists only in the imagination or an ultimate goal or aim

idealist – someone who envisions a perfect world rather than perceiving the real one, is often naive and impractical, and typically thinks in terms of social responsibility and social justice, often with little or no consideration to logical inconsistencies, means, or cost

identify – to recognize as a particular person or thing

identity – the distinguishing beliefs, characteristics, or qualities of a person or group of people

ignorant – having no knowledge, the condition of being unaware or uninformed

ill-considered – unwise or foolish, not showing careful thought

illegal – forbidden by law or edict

illogical – contradicting or disregarding the principles of logic

illusion – a mistaken perception of reality

imagination – the faculty to form a mental perception of something that has never before been known to actually exist

imagine – the act or instance of forming a perception of something in one's mind

immeasurable – impossible to measure or without known limits

immoral – not in accord with moral standards

immunity – circumstance of being protected from typical consequence

impact – to have direct effect

impartial – lack of preference for one thing over another

imperfect – characterized by defects or weaknesses

implication – the effect a decision, action, or event is logically expected to have on something else

important – something that is necessary or that has significant worth or value

impose – to force on another or others

impossible – cannot exist or occur

impractical – not practical or useful

impression – an indistinct but consequential notion or remembrance

improper – not appropriate, suitable, or correct

impulsive – acting suddenly without planning or consideration

inaccurate – incorrect or untrue

incentive – a reward offered to encourage one to do something, an extrinsic inducement that can or does incite determination or action

incite – to move or provoke to action

inclination – a preference for thinking or acting in a particular way

inclusive – available and open to all

incremental – denoting a usually small positive or negative change in a variable quantity

incremental incentive – an incitement to act that is characterized by the incremental benefits of taking action exceeding its incremental costs

independence of mind – belief that individual freedom and the virtues of self-reliance and personal independence should be favored over collective or state control

independent – free from dominance or control of others, relying on one's own judgment, capabilities, or resources

individual – reference to a single human being or other single distinct entity

individualism – belief that individual freedom and the virtues of self-reliance and personal independence should be favored over collective or state control

indoctrination – continuously repeating and promoting a doctrine, principle, or ideology until it is accepted without doubt as being true

induce – to move by persuasion or influence

indulgent – benignly lenient or permissive

inevitable – impossible to avoid or prevent, certain to happen

inference – the act of reasoning based on knowledge or evidence

influence – a power to change a someone's belief or behavior or to affect a course of events without exerting direct control or apparent effort

influence peddling – use of real or potential influence on someone's behalf in exchange for money or favors

information – facts or ideas received or given

informed – the condition of being aware, knowledgeable, or educated

infringe – to encroach upon or breach the boundary of something

inherent – existing as something inseparable from the whole

injure – to cause harm or inflict damage

injustice – unfair, morally wrong

innate – something that naturally exists at the beginning of life

innovation – change that creates a new dimension of performance

insider trading – the act of basing personal investment decisions on confidential or privileged information

insignificant – lacking importance, not worth considering

instance – a happening or occurrence of something

instinct – an innate response to specific stimuli, how one naturally behaves, thinks, or feels

institution – a significant and established organization

institutional – relating to or affecting an entire organization or culture, or fundamental to a social, economic, or political practice

insufficient – lacking in what is necessary or required

integrate – to unite or bring parts together to form a whole

integrity – unwavering adherence to a moral standard or ethical code

intellect – a person's capacity for learning, thinking, and understanding

intelligent – having or showing the capacity or ability to reason and understand

intense – existing in a high or extreme degree

intent – desire or will to do something

interact – to act reciprocally or one upon another

interaction – mutual or reciprocal action or influence

interdependent – influenced or impacted by each other

interest – concern about or involvement with something or someone; something that arouses curiosity or draws attention

internal – things that exist or happen inside a person or thing

interpersonal skills – abilities related to the emotional or cognitive activities of an individual concerning self, specifically self-awareness of one's own talents, beliefs, values, and attitude, and the effect such awareness has on one's decisions, behavior, and point of view

interrelated – the condition of a thing having an effect or dependency on the other

interrupt – to stop or cause a break in continuity

intervene – to come between or interfere

intrinsic – relating to the essential nature of a person or thing

introvert – a person who is inclined to limit social engagement or embraces a greater than average preference for solitude

intuition – what one feels to be true or correct, often without any conscious reasoning or proof

investment – an asset acquired for the purpose of producing future wealth

invigorating – the quality of having an enlivening or stimulating effect

involve – to have a part or be included in something

irresponsible – not accountable for own conduct; not dependable or trustworthy

journalist – a person engaged in collecting, writing, editing, and presenting news or news articles

joy – a feeling of delight or elation

judge – to form an opinion after careful consideration; to consider or decide a legal matter or consequence

judgment – the ability to make considered decisions or come to sensible conclusions; a decision or position arrived at by reasoning from premises or general principles

judgmental – being quick to criticize the actions of others, often without understanding the reasons for their beliefs or behavior

judicial – pertaining to courts of law or administration of justice

judicious – having, showing, or done using good judgment or common sense

just – conforming to a standard of fair treatment and due reward

justice – concept of fair treatment and due reward that relies on laws under which all people are treated equally

justifiable – having proof or sufficient reason to believe that something is right or valid

justify – to show or prove that something is right or valid

know – to perceive or understand with clarity or certainty; to be familiar with or have knowledge of

knowledge – information acquired through experience, schooling, or study

known – perceived or understood with clarity or certainty; the condition of having familiarity or knowledge

labor unions – organizations that represent the collective interests of union members, often with legally protected and government-promoted monopolistic power

later – at a subsequent time

lawful – allowed or not prohibited by law

laws of nature – the uniformity of natural instincts, actions, and relationships of organic beings

leader – one who shows the way and persuades others to follow; the person who is in charge

leadership – the ability to influence and guide others toward achieving a common objective

learn – to acquire knowledge or skill or to become aware and informed

legal – relating to or concerned with law; established or recognized by law

legitimate – in compliance with laws or accepted rules and standards; reasonable and acceptable

lenient – merciful, not harsh or severe

lie – a statement made with deliberate intent to deceive

life – aspect of organic existence which grows and evolves; the span of time an organism is alive; all of the experiences and actions that constitute a person's existence

likely – probably will happen or is expected to happen

limit – something that bounds, restricts, or restrains

link – to connect one thing with another

live – to be alive or to reside in a particular place

logical – relating to or in accordance with reasoning that involves correct or reliable inference

logical thinking – cognition that is fact-based and logical

logically inconsistent – a set of assertions, ideas, statements, or the like that cannot all be true at the same time; an unresolvable contradiction between parts of an argument

loyal – faithful to a person or cause, steadfast in allegiance

lucid – plainly expressed and easy to comprehend

luck – the chance happening of good fortune or adversity

malicious – intentionally and purposefully causing harm

market – a gathering where buyers and sellers exchange goods and services

market economy – an economic system that relies mostly on market forces to determine prices and allocate resources and goods and services

mass media – the microcosm of journalists and advertising professionals, and entertainment, professional sports, and media celebrities

material – something that is used or that can be used to make something else; having importance or consequence

mathematical aptitude – capacity to understand mathematical operations, and more broadly, the capacity to analyze situations and solve problems logically

maximize – to increase as much as possible

meaningful – having function or purpose

means – method or way and resources used or needed to do something

measure – an adequate or suitable proportion or amount; to ascertain the quantity or quality of something

media – members of the mass media

memory – the mental faculty of retaining and recalling what has been experienced and learned

mental – relating to the mind

mentor – a wise and trusted counselor and teacher

merit – demonstrated value, ability, or achievement

meritocracy – a social system, society, or organization in which individual personal success is dependent on demonstrated value, ability, or achievement rather than on social class, credentials, intent, tenure, personal connections, privilege, or celebrity

method – a procedure, technique, or way of doing something

methodical – acting or proceeding in an orderly and precise way

microcosm – a small community or society

mind – the faculty of a person that enables one to perceive, think, remember, desire, and imagine

mislead – to give a wrong impression or guide toward a wrong conclusion

misrepresent – to describe or depict something falsely or incorrectly

modest – having or showing a restrained or moderate opinion of one's own capabilities or achievements

modify – to make generally minor adjustments in something

money – medium of exchange with unit value equal to the goods and services that can be acquired for it

monopoly – enterprise that is able, at least in the short term, to cause economic results different from what would otherwise occur in a free market by dominating the market for goods and services it produces or delivers

moral – adhering to standards of responsible, respectful, and fair behavior

morality – relating to or concerned with the standards of personal behavior

morals – a society's rules or standards for desirable or acceptable personal behavior

morph – to change or transform over time from one thing to another

motivation – the interests and concerns of a person which determine attitude and behavior

motive – reason a person does something or considers doing something

movement – motion or development

multidimensional – having two or more spatial aspects or important or prominent parts

multinational business enterprises – companies with substantial business operations spread across different countries

multiple – more than one

mutual – shared in common

mutually exclusive – not possible to occur or exist at the same time

naive – lacking knowledge, comprehension, or concern; unaware or unsuspecting

nation – a territorially bounded sovereign political entity ruled in the name of a community of citizens who identify themselves as an independent country

natural – existing in or formed by nature

nature – the material world and its phenomena; the inherent character or basic constitution of a person or thing

necessary – needed or required

need – something that is required or necessary

negative – not expecting good things to happen; undesirable, unfavorable, or detrimental; characterized by subtraction or decrease

normal – something considered to be usual or typical or without abnormalities or deficiencies

notion – vague or imprecise impression or idea

obedience – bending to the will or authority of another

object – the focus of attention, feeling, thought, or action; something material that may be perceived by the senses

objective – the quality or condition of not being influenced by personal beliefs or feelings in considering and representing facts; a goal toward which effort is directed

obligation – a course of action to which one is morally or legally constrained

occupation – an activity in which one regularly engages as a means to obtain the necessities of life

occupy – to fill, exist in, or use; to engage one's attention or energies

occur – to happen or take place

offense – a violation or infraction of law or moral standard

open-minded – willing to consider new and different ideas or the opinions of others

operate – to perform or function

operation – the process or series of acts required to do something; some form of work or production

opinion – belief about something that may or may not be based on fact or knowledge

opportunity – a situation which makes it possible to do something in particular

oppose – to be in conflict with or act against

opposites – a duality of complementary or mutually exclusive things

optimistic – inclined to take a positive view of events or conditions and expect favorable outcomes

option – an alternative course of action that can be chosen from a set of possibilities; the opportunity to choose

order – a state of peace, freedom from confused or unruly behavior; arrangement or disposition of people, things, or events in relation to each other

organic – pertaining to or derived from living beings

organism – any living thing

organization – a group of people who work together in a structured way for a particular purpose; spontaneous or deliberate formation of arrangement or order

original – the first instance of something

originate – to come into or bring into being

outcome – a consequence, end result, or final product

overall – in general rather than in particular

overconfidence – excessive or unjustified trust in one's judgment or abilities

parasitic – existing at the expense of others, often causing great harm and contributing nothing of value in return

pardon – to excuse an offense without exacting a penalty or punishment

partial – bias toward or preference for one thing over another

participant – a person who becomes involved or takes part in something

participate – to be active or involved in something

particular – reference to a single person or thing rather than to others

partisan – a ardent supporter or advocate of a party, faction, or cause

pattern – an arrangement or sequence that repeats in a predictable way

peace – freedom from disturbance

peculiar – belonging only or primarily to a single individual or group of individuals

peer – person who has equal standing

people skills – ability to communicate effectively, work collaboratively, and build worthwhile relationships with others

perceive – to sense, recognize, realize, or understand

perception – comprehension or understanding of something

perceptive – having or showing keen insight, understanding, or intuition

perfect – the unattainable state or condition of being without any fault or defect

performance – action of doing something or competence demonstrated when doing it

permanent – lasting or remaining without change

person – an individual human being

personal – anything that relates or pertains to an individual person's own self

personal resources – the physical body, mind, energy, and time that are naturally and uniquely possessed by each human being

personal responsibility – the idea that all people should be accountable for their own decisions and actions

personality – the qualities and traits that are peculiar to a particular human or non-human animal

persuade – to convince someone to accept a point of view or to act by means of example, explanation, discussion, or debate

pessimistic – inclined to take a negative view of events or conditions and expect unfavorable outcomes

phenomenon – an observable fact or event

philosophy – the study of human values and knowledge; a system of thought

physical – relating to the material structure of organic beings; having material or concrete existence

planned economy – an economic system that relies mostly on government agencies to allocate goods and resources and determine prices

play – to engage in an activity for amusement or recreation

pleasure – a feeling of gladness or being pleased

plunder – to steal or take wrongfully

point of view – the perspective from which we view and explain something

political – relating to public affairs and governance

political patronage – appointment or hiring of someone on the basis of partisan loyalty to fill a government position

politician – person who is professionally involved in politics, especially as a holder of or a candidate for an elected office or a political appointee

position – one's role and importance in an organization or in society; a person's firm belief or point of view

positive – full of hope and confidence; desirable, beneficial, or constructive; characterized by increase or addition

possess – to have under one's power or control

possible – can happen or be done

potential – capable of being but not yet in existence

power – being able to do what one wants; having the ability to control people or things; force required to produce an effect

practical – concerned with the actual doing of something or in fact being useful rather than with theory and ideas

practice – something done regularly or constantly

precedence – the condition of having higher priority

predator – one that injures, exploits, or plunders others

preference – the fact of liking, wanting, or choosing one thing rather than another

prejudice – having or showing an unfair or unreasonable opinion or feeling, especially when formed without logical thought and relevant knowledge

preoccupy – to dominate one's mind or attention

prescribe – to mandate as a rule or course of action to be followed

prevent – to stop something from occurring

previous – coming or occurring before whatever is next in time or order

prey – one that is the victim of another

price – the amount paid for goods or services

pride – a feeling of pleasure or satisfaction taken in an achievement, possession, or association; feeling or showing justifiable self-esteem

primacy – the condition or state of being first or foremost

primary – of greatest importance or most significant

prime element – fundamental or most critical component of a complex entity

principal – most important or consequential

principle – a rule or standard of action or conduct; a fundamental truth that serves as a foundational tenet of a system of beliefs or a chain of reasoning

principled – consistently acting in accord with one's own code of ethical conduct

priority – the state or fact of being more important; the relative position assigned to something

privilege – special entitlement granted to an individual or group that benefits only the individual or group and not society as a whole

privileged – available or limited to only one or a few

problem – an issue or question to be considered, solved, or answered

problematic – to cause or be full of difficulties

process – a series of actions or changes; a series of tasks done to accomplish a particular result

produce – to bring about or create

production – act of using, combining, or processing various raw materials and other capital resources to create goods and services

productive – achieving or creating something of significant value

productivity – the quality, state, or fact of being able to create, enhance, or provide goods and services; rate or efficiency with which various resources are used in producing goods and services

professional – relating to work that requires special training or exceptional skill; engaged in an activity as an occupation

progress – movement toward improved quality of life and standard of living

progressive – one who believes in enforcing social equality through vigorous governmental action

prohibit – to officially forbid or refuse to allow something

projection – falsely and maliciously claiming that one's own beliefs or point of view are those of another person or group of people

prominent – well-known or easily seen

promote – to help or encourage to exist or flourish; to raise to a more important or responsible job or higher rank

propaganda – information, especially of a prejudiced, misleading, or untrue nature, used to promote or publicize a particular cause or point of view

proper – appropriate, suitable, or correct

property – anything legally owned by an individual person, including ownership of oneself and a right to personal well-being

property rights – legal protections that enable people and legal entities to own, use, and receive benefits from tangible and intangible resources and economic goods

proposition – something offered for consideration, acceptance, or adoption

prosper – to have success or financial well-being

prosperity – the condition of being wealthy or successful

protect – to defend or shield against injury, harm, or loss

provide – to make available or to supply

prudent – wise or judicious, careful in providing for the future

psychological – relating to the mind

psychology – the study of individual human thought and behavior

publicize – to cause public awareness

purport – to have or present an often false appearance or intention

purpose – the objective toward which one strives or for which something exists

purposefully – mindful of the objective toward which one strives

quality – a characteristic or the essential nature of a person or thing; level of excellence

quality of life – a subjective assessment of overall enjoyment of life

quantity – the amount or total number of something

range – a grouping of things; the extent of variation

rank – the relative position or status of a person or thing; to place in sequential order

rational – relating to or involving reason or knowledge; logical or sensible

react – to respond to a stimulus

reaction – the natural or learned response to various stimuli

realist – a person who accepts and deals practically with things as they are and who typically thinks in terms of personal responsibility, incentives and constraints, social processes, options, and relative costs

realistic – having an awareness of things as they actually are rather than as they are imagined or desired to be

reality – the state of things as they actually are rather than as they are imagined or desired to be

reason – the ability of the human mind to think, understand, and form judgments by a process of logic; the basis or motive for an action, decision, or belief

reasonable – as much as is appropriate, fair, or sensible, not excessive

reasoning – using one's mind to think, understand, and form judgments

reciprocal – an equivalent or similar action done in response to another's action

recreation – physical or mental activity engaged in primarily for fun

recur – happening or appearing repeatedly

reduce – to make or become smaller

refute – to show or prove that something is false or erroneous

regard – careful consideration or attention

regret – an all-things-considered feeling of sadness, distress, or remorse for one's actions or behavior

regular – usual, normal, or customary; recurring at fixed or uniform intervals

relate – to have connection or reference

relationship – the state of being related or interrelated; a connection, association, or involvement

relative – considered in comparison or relation to something else

relax – to reduce in intensity, make less severe or strict

relevant – having significant and demonstrable bearing on something happening or being considered

reliable – accurate or trustworthy

religion – faith-based organizations or institutions structured around common beliefs in and reverence for a supernatural power or powers

religious – having strong belief in and reverence for a deity or deities

relinquish – to give up possession or control

rely – to depend on or place trust in

remedy – to correct or counteract

representative – something that is typical of or similar to other things of a type or group; a system of governance in which members of a governmental body, usually legislative, are chosen by popular vote to make laws that advance the common interests of their constituents

republicanism – a representative form of government in which the civil liberties that are guaranteed to every citizen are codified in a constitution

required – stipulated as absolutely indispensable

resent – to feel displeased or aggrieved due to a sense of being treated unjustly

resource – something that has utility or that is available for use

respectful – feeling or showing due regard and tolerance for self and others

responsibility – the condition of being obligated to deal with something or being accountable for something

responsible – accountable for own conduct; dependable and trustworthy

restrict – to keep within specified boundaries

result – to occur as a consequence, effect, or conclusion

reverence – a feeling or attitude of awe and deep respect

right – conforms with ethical and moral principles; an entitlement to which each person has an equal moral or legal claim; correct or accurate

rights – entitlements to which each person has an equal moral or legal claim

risk – the condition of potentially suffering harm or loss

role – functional part or element of something

rule – the exercise of authority or control; a standard of judgment or action

rule of law – principle of governance that restricts the arbitrary exercise of governmental control by subordinating it to well-defined and established laws under which all people are treated equally

rule of man – principle of governance that prescribed government action be based on circumstances of situation as decided arbitrarily by ruling authority

ruler – one who exercises controlling power over others

ruling class – relatively small group of people who decide upon a society's political structure and agenda

satisfaction – feeling pleased about accomplishing a goal, meeting an expectation, or fulfilling a need

satisfactory – fully sufficient to meet a demand or requirement

scarce – small, insignificant, or insufficient amount

scaremongering – the action of creating or spreading stories that make people feel worried or fearful

scope – extent of consideration, activity, or influence

security – free from actual risk or danger

seek – to strive to obtain

self – the total, essential, or particular being of an individual human

self-absorbed – preoccupied with one's own wants and needs and not caring about the needs or feelings of others

self-aware – aware of oneself, including one's capabilities, traits, feelings, beliefs, and behaviors

self-centered – concerned solely or chiefly with one's own advantage, pleasure, or well-being

self-esteem – one's sense of one's own worth and value

self-interested – concerned for one's own advantage and well-being

self-preservation – the basic instinct of preserving one's own existence'

selfless – having no concern for one's own advantage or well-being

sense – a feeling or perception; conscious awareness or rationality

senses – faculties, such as sight, hearing, smell, taste, or touch, by which humans perceive external and internal stimuli

sensible – practical, acting in accordance with wisdom or prudence

separate – to be apart or independent

series – a group of objects coming one after the other

set – a group of similar or related things

significant – important and deserving of attention

similar – having common but not identical characteristics

situation – a state of affairs; the circumstances and what is occurring at a particular time and place

skeptical – a doubting or questioning attitude or state of mind

skill – learned ability to do something in an efficient and capable way

social – relating to the way people live together and interact with others

social class – a group of people of similar status, rank, or common characteristics within a society who possess the same socioeconomic status

social equality – socially progressive and arguably logically impossible idea of assuring equal outcomes for all people of different genders, classes, races, ethnicities, nationalities, sexual orientations, abilities, disabilities, and the like

social institution – an entity formed to meet a societal need or preserve a societal value

social justice – a socially progressive concept of fair and just relations between the individual and society that commits to providing to all equal wealth, opportunities for personal activity, and social privileges

social order – the system of institutions, structures, and organizing principles that are used to maintain society

social philosophy – view of how personal and societal responsibilities and rights should be prioritized

social processes – the ways in which individuals and groups typically interact and form social relationships

social responsibility – socially progressive idea that all people who have an ability to affect change that they believe is beneficial to society also have an obligation to make use of that ability however they can

socialism – a political and social philosophy based originally on the principles of collectivism that has now morphed into an authoritarian political system that characteristically exercises tight control over political, social, and economic affairs

socialization – the process of acquiring the values, habits, and attitudes of a society

society – a system of human organization that supplies protection, continuity, security, and identity; a group of people who live as interdependent members of a community

socioeconomic – relating to both social and economic factors

sociology – the study of human social behavior

sociopolitical – relating to or involving both social and political factors

solitude – the state or quality of being alone

solve – to find a solution, explanation, or answer to a problem or issue

sound – without defect as to truth, wisdom, or reason

space – the three-dimensional area in which all matter exists

spatial – relating to the relative position, area, and size of things

special – exceptional, surpassing what is common or usual

species – a group of closely related animals or plants which have common attributes

specific – relating to a particular person or thing; explicitly and clearly set forth

specify – to identify or to state clearly

spiritual – feeling, sense, or belief the world is affected by something that is cosmic or divine

spontaneous – happening or arising without apparent external cause

stability – firmness in position

stage – one of a series of steps or positions

standard – an established or acceptable measure of value, quality, or quantity; a basis of comparison

standard of living – the level of material comfort experienced by a person or group of people

state – the whole being of something; a politically organized body of people

state of mind – relating to state of a person's emotional and cognitive processes

statement – a description, assertion, or declaration

status – relative social, professional, or other standing of a person or thing

steadfast – firmly loyal or constant, fixed or unswerving

stimulate – to encourage or cause a spurt in activity, growth, or development

stipulate – to specify, demand, or concede something in particular

stipulative definition – purports to describe the commonly accepted meaning of a term, but actually specifies an uncommon or altered use

strawman definition – a misrepresented or distorted position or opinion that is easier to attack or refute than the original and actual position or opinion

strength – the state or quality of having physical power or capacity

strict – stringent in requirement or control

strive – to exert significant effort to accomplish

structure – the composition of something that is made from parts; the way parts are put together to form a whole

study – applying the mind to the acquisition of knowledge through reading, observation, or research

stupid – the quality or state of not exercising or showing sound judgment

subjective – influenced by or based on beliefs and feelings

submission – yielding or submitting to dominant power

submit – to yield to governance, authority, or will of another

subordinate – subject to the authority of another

success – favorable or desirable outcome; accomplishment of something desired, planned, or attempted

successful – the condition of having done something desired, planned, or attempted

successive – following in order without interruption

sufficient – having as much as is needed

superior – excellent of its kind or of higher in rank, quality, or importance

supernatural – relating to existence outside the natural world

supply – quantity or amount that is needed or available; to provide or make available

support – to serve as a foundation; to provide substantiation; to supply the necessities of life

suppress – to curtail or prevent something from being seen or expressed

survive – to remain alive

system – interacting, interrelated, or interdependent elements that form or function as a whole

systematic – methodical, characterized by thoroughness and regularity

systemic – relating to the inherent interdependencies of a system

systemic causation – a causation in which interdependent events or things interact and reciprocally affect one another and sometimes transform into events or things that did not previously exist

systemic rationality – the idea that knowledge and reasons that are unknowable to any individual participant spontaneously produce through systemic interaction reasonable decisions and outcomes for the whole

talent – an exceptional aptitude or ability to do something

task – a discrete piece of work

tendency – disposition to think or act in a particular way

tenet – one of two or more principles upon which a belief or theory is based

tenure – the length of time that a person remains in a position or job

term – a word or expression that when used contextually has precise meaning

theoretical – existing only in theory, lacking actual existence

theory – an abstract idea that is possibly true, but is not proven to be true

think – to use one's mind to remember, ponder, imagine, plan, decide, or otherwise produce thought

thinking – the act of using one's mind to produce thought

thorough – exhaustively complete, without negligence or omissions

thoughtful – characterized by or deliberate and careful thinking; showing consideration for others

three-dimensional – having the dimensions of depth, width, and height

thrive – to be successful or to flourish

time – the indefinite continuance of the past, present, and future; a non-renewable and ultimately finite resource that can be expended in alternative ways and has greatest value in the present

time and place – unique and virtually immeasurable number of combinations of points in time and space

tolerance – patient indulgence with beliefs or behaviors of others that are different from one's own

tolerate – to permit something to exist without prohibition or interference

total – the whole amount or complete scope of something

tradition – time-honored institutions and established customs

trait – a genetically determined characteristic

transform – to change in appearance, composition, or structure

treat – to deal with something or someone in a particular way

tribalism – a sociopolitical organization that is united by ties of common ancestry, customs, and traditions

trickery – pretense or crafty ingenuity to deceive or cheat

true – that which exists in accordance with fact or reality

trust – confident reliance on character, ability, strength, or integrity

trustworthy – deserving of trust or confidence

turmoil – a state of great commotion, confusion, or agitation

two-tiered justice – refers to a judicial system in which some people are granted greater legal immunity or are judged more leniently than others

typical – the generally common characteristics or behavior of a group of people or things

ultimate – most extreme or important; last in a series, process, or progression

ultimately – in the end or eventually

unacceptable – not suitable to meet a need or standard

unachievable – impossible to achieve

unavoidable – not possible to be avoided, inevitable

understand – to comprehend the nature, significance, or explanation of something

understanding – the condition or quality of having the ability to comprehend and judge the nature and significance of something

unexpected – not anticipated nor thought likely

unfair – characterized by injustice, partiality, or deception

unfavorable – not favorable or advantageous

uniform – always the same, identical or consistent in form, manner, or degree

unique – existing as the only one, implies being without a known parallel

unit – an individual, group, structure, or other entity regarded as a primary element of a whole

unity – a state or condition of oneness or standing together; being in agreement or in accord

unknowable – impossible to know, existing beyond the capacities of human cognition or knowledge

unknown – not within the scope of one's knowledge, experience, or understanding

unlawful – not allowed by law

unlimited – having no restrictions or boundaries

unscrupulous – unprincipled and dishonest

untrue – not true, contrary to fact, false

unwavering – characterized by firm and steady determination or resolve

use – to put into action or service or employ for a purpose

useful – helpful, suited to purpose

usual – what most often happens or most often is done

utility – the quality of being useful

valid – based on truth or reason

value – the usefulness or importance of someone or something

values – personal beliefs that guide individual behavior

variable – the quality of being able or likely to change

verbal aptitude – capacity to reason using concepts framed in words, crucial to abstract thinking, working memory, and written and spoken communication

victim – one that is harmed by another

view – an opinion, belief, or idea, or a way of thinking about something; extent or range of vision

violate – to act in a manner that is unlawful or immoral

virtually – in fact or for all practical purposes; almost but not quite, nearly

virtue – moral excellence; an admirable quality or trait

visual-spatial aptitude – capacity to identify, integrate, and analyze visual forms and multidimensional spatial relationships

vital – extremely significant and important; necessary for existence or well-being

vocabulary – fundamental tool for communication and acquiring knowledge; all words used or known by a particular person

vocation – an occupation to which one is particularly attracted

voluntary – done willingly without expectation of reward

waste – to use or expend needlessly or carelessly

wealthy – the state or condition of having significant resources

welfare – physical and mental health and happiness

well-being – a satisfactory state or condition

well-defined – clearly and unambiguously stated

whole – all aspects of a thing, something in its entirety

wisdom – sound judgment based on a deep and perceptive understanding of reality

wise – having or showing sound judgment based on a deep and perceptive understanding of reality

wish – to have a desire or longing for something that is difficult to obtain or is unattainable

word – a unit of language that conveys meaning

work – mental or physical effort expended to accomplish or produce something; to function or operate

world – the earthly state of human existence

worth – the character or intrinsic qualities of someone or something

worthwhile – sufficiently valuable to justify investment of time, effort, or interest

wrong – not in accord with ethical and moral principles; untrue or incorrect

yield – to give up control of or responsibility for something

www.ingramcontent.com/pod-product-compliance
Lightning Source LLC
Chambersburg PA
CBHW070531090426
42735CB00013B/2942